50 After 50

"Maria Olsen has opened her heart in this deeply personal story that travels from deep despair through an affirming journey to renewal and joy. A compelling story that offers advice and encouragement for anyone seeking purpose, passion, and happiness." **—Robin Gerber**, author of *Leadership the Eleanor Roosevelt Way: Timeless Strategies from the First Lady of Courage* and *Katharine Graham: The Leadership Journey of an American Icon*

"Olsen is provocatively honest in her new book, *50 After 50*, as she openly talks about delicate topics from her past. I applaud her ability to re-create herself and seek her bliss. This book shows how we can all change our mindset and transform ourselves if we choose. I highly recommend this book for anyone seeking their best life." **—Trish Earnest**, addictions clinician and author of *Blood on the Walls: A Woman's Journey From Rebellion to Redemption*

"I am so glad Olsen is mapping out her explorations and encouraging other women to go on their own adventures. I work with a lot of women who turn 50 and say *What now? What's next? Who am I?* I love the idea of explorations, experiments, and deep dives during this beautiful stage in life. What a gift to have this conversation. Aging is really the privilege of a lifetime." **—Pleasance Silicki**, health coach, teacher, and author of *Delight: Eight Principles for Living with Joy and Ease*

"Olsen has the courage and knows the importance of conquering fears, fulfilling dreams, and taking new steps at every stage of life. I'd follow her anywhere!" **—Iris Krasnow**, best-selling author of relationship books

"It feels like a miracle! Just as I am entering the final countdown to 50 myself, embarking on a career change, and as our youngest child has left for school, Olsen, who I have long admired, sent me her delectable manuscript. This book is now cherished reading and a guidebook to the next chapter of my life. As soon as I put it down I'll be starting my own '50 after 50' list and will get busy checking them off!" **—Aviva Goldfarb**, author and entrepreneur; founder of The Six O'Clock Scramble

50 After 50

Reframing the Next
Chapter of Your Life

Maria Leonard Olsen

ROWMAN & LITTLEFIELD
Lanham • Boulder • New York • London

Published by Rowman & Littlefield
A wholly owned subsidary of The Rowman & Littlefield Publishing Group, Inc.
4501 Forbes Boulevard, Suite 200, Lanham, Maryland 20706
www.rowman.com

Unit A, Whitacre Mews, 26-34 Stannary Street, London SE11 4AB

British Library Cataloguing in Publication Information Available

Library of Congress Cataloging-in-Publication Data

Names: Olsen, Maria Leonard, author.
Title: 50 after 50 : reframing the next chapter of your life / Maria Leonard Olsen.
Other titles: Fifty after fifty
Description: Lanham : Rowman & Littlefield, [2018] | Includes bibliographical references and index.
Identifiers: LCCN 2017052855 (print) | LCCN 2017054665 (ebook) | ISBN 9781538109656 (Electronic) | ISBN 9781538109649 (cloth : alk. paper)
Subjects: LCSH: Middle age—Psychological aspects. | Change (Psychology) | Rejuvenation. | Aging—Psychological aspects.
Classification: LCC BF724.6 (ebook) | LCC BF724.6 .O47 2018 (print) | DDC 155.67/19—dc23
LC record available at https://lccn.loc.gov/2017052855

Printed in the United States of America

To my sisters in sobriety,
especially Sandy, the woman who helped save me from myself

Contents

Preface

Maria 2.0, or Out of the
Mud Comes the Lotus

$\mathcal{A}$t age 50, I drank my way out of my 25-year marriage. I had, against advice I knew, put all my eggs in the motherhood basket, willfully derailing my successful law career. As teenagers, my precious children did not need me in the hands-on way they had previously. In fact, they were "dirtying the nest" in preparation for going off to college and beyond. My husband and I had grown apart because, among other things that were entirely my fault, we failed to nurture that important relationship. I was depressed and stuck.

As I turned 50, I had the distinct feeling that I was on the downward slope of my life. Actuarially speaking, I was. So when I turned 50, my gift to myself was to go on a crusade to make the most of whatever time I had left. I set out to do 50 new things that were, perhaps, significant only to me. The list spanned physical challenges, adventure, travel, spiritual work, and lifestyle changes. Each taught me something about myself and how I wanted to live the next decade and more of my life.

We all have challenges in life and cards we are dealt that we would rather not face. Life does not go as planned. But each of us can adapt and reshape our circumstances moving forward.

I had a lot of darkness in my past. It was painful to come to terms with some of that. But I took the necessary steps for me to heal. I have heard that the lotus flower grows out of mud. It took me a long time to appreciate my mud. . . .

I had always been a bit of a dilettante. I was fairly good at many things, but expert at none. Part of that had to do with my desire to evade introspection. I spent much of my life running away from myself—running so fast so that I would not have time to look within. When my therapist asked me what made me happy, aside from my children, I had no answer. When I reflect on this now, I am astounded. I suppose I really did not know who I was in any meaningful way. For the most part, I just took on roles that were expected of me and subjugated my desires unless they coincided or meshed with the given role. Pursuing 50 new things was part of my quest to determine who I was at my core and what cultivated joy for me.

The definition of happiness is debatable. In my youth, it meant pleasure and excitement. Those things can contribute to happiness, but I was looking for something less fleeting. At 50, happiness for me means contentment, serenity, and peace—with some spice mixed in.

I set off on a spiritual retreat, to search for clues about the authentic me and the meaning of my life. I actually went to rehab first, which was spiritual—so spiritual that I went five times. What planted the seeds of my transformation was a retreat led by don Miguel Ruiz in Teotihuacan, Mexico.[1] I now strive to live my life according to the tenets of his book, *The Four Agreements*.[2] These "Four Agreements" and the Twelve Steps[3] for recovering alcoholics provided the road map for the next chapter of my life.

So eager was I to share my new way of living that I joined forces with friend, Dr. Nicole Cutts, and led some writers' spiritual/empowerment retreats. Our tribe of women writers and seekers continues to support each other and check in on our writing and other projects. Participants have called our Vision Quest Writing Retreats[4] "healing and affirming," and "full of love, authenticity, and breakthrough."

I came to terms with being middle-aged. I didn't actually like the way I looked in the mirror, so I looked in the mirror less. I had been a lifelong athlete of some sort, and had run three marathons. The fire for running had dimmed since nearing and turning 50, and my knees rebelled at the beatings they had taken. I took up walking, and run-walking. I took more time appreciating nature as I moved along. I did daily gratitude lists in my mind and on paper. I prayed, sometimes reciting rosaries in my mind.

After I made some headway on my spiritual path, I set out to try new adventures. One of the more radical things I chose in this new chapter of my life—and most horrifying to my children—was to get my motorcycle license and a motorcycle after training at a local Harley-Davidson dealership. My now ex-husband got himself a Maserati at about the same time (but that's a different story). This is my story.

I have some trepidation over revealing so much of my own dirty laundry, but part of my quest is to be open, to have no secrets, and to live in the light. Secrets can keep us sick. It is also cathartic for me to get everything out and to channel my learning in positive ways. I can now acknowledge that all mistakes and experiences present opportunities for learning if we are honest, open, and willing.

I hope my journey inspires you and other women to drink fully from the cup of life, maybe even earlier than I did. Time is a precious and finite commodity. Don't waste it.

After decades of simmering self-hatred, I can honestly say that I like Maria 2.0. May you find your next version now.

I

WHY I DID THIS
(AND WHY YOU SHOULD, TOO)

$\mathscr{D}$ays can be long, but years seem to be getting shorter and shorter as I age. The fact that I have lost more loved ones in recent years has made me more acutely aware of my mortality, and incited an urgency in me to not waste whatever time I have left on this planet. Just this week, a healthy college classmate of mine fell, struck his head, and died instantly. Almost a dozen of my friends have been diagnosed with breast cancer, and several died from the disease. I believe life gives us wake-up calls. I no longer choose to ignore them.

What brought me to this point of critical self-evaluation and recalibration? It took me a long time to accept myself as perfectly imperfect. I carried much baggage that negatively affected my life until I dealt with it properly. I reached a crisis stage that forced me to realign my priorities and take a hard look at where my life was heading. I wish I had not allowed such chaos into my life, but it brought me to where I am now. For that, I am grateful.

I began as a biracial child whose parents were forbidden by law to marry in the state of Maryland in the early 1960s. I tried desperately to fit into an overwhelmingly white tableau, compromising large parts of my identity. I excelled at school and made my way through a top-ten law school, achieved a certain amount of success at a large D.C. law firm, and was granted a political appointment in the Clinton administration's Department of Justice. Maternal instincts outweighed professional aspirations, and I became the mother of two amazing children. Perfectionism was my goal as a stay-at-home mom, and I read every book on the subject, researching and practicing motherhood as exhaustively as I would have treated cases in my former legal practice. I strove to create the type of childhood for my children about which I had yearned and fantasized.

1

After years of this, I snapped. Alcoholism flared and I lost most of what I had built, including an almost 25-year marriage, a beautiful home in one of Washington's most exclusive suburbs, and other trappings of wealth and privilege. My kids grew up and did not need me in the day-to-day way I had devoted myself to for nearly two decades. So I went back to the working world and started over, in many ways. Now, I'm a life adventurer, making the most of whatever time I have left.

Everyone has something in their life that is a challenge. Many of us, especially women who have been socialized to assume caretaker roles, are not adept at handling competing demands on our time. In a social media–frenzied society, it often appears that everyone else lives picture-perfect lives with ease. They do not. Life coaching has become a lucrative industry. Books on how to be happy have proliferated the nation's bookshelves. We all could use some help.

I had some major skeletons to deal with before I could stop running from them and live according to my values. I thought pretending I was someone else and ignoring these issues would be enough. But it was not. Until I dealt with the problems straight on, I would continue to suffer in silence and hide myself behind an armored persona I had built.

After I faced the skeletons I had buried, my life improved tremendously. My quest to try 50 new things after my 50th birthday was a celebration and extension of this improvement. When we enter our fifth decade, many of us have more free time, resources, and life experience to take on empowerment activities such as those suggested in this book. We do not have to allow societal patterns to dictate any sort of decline toward retirement.

Take a look at what I had to deal with before I could start my quest. And try not to judge me. We all have dirt. It just takes different forms.

Ernest Hemingway is attributed with saying, "There is nothing to writing. All you do is sit down to a typewriter and bleed."[1] I have bled all over these pages. I hid many of these secrets for so long and attempt now to walk through the fear with the hope of helping you do the same.

• 1 •

Recovering from Childhood

$\mathcal{W}$e all have baggage. For most of us, at least some of that baggage is residue from childhood. Here's mine.

As much as we hate to admit it, childhood experiences affect us throughout our lives. Some of us, even unwittingly so, repeat the sins of our parents. Others rebel against them. I did a bit of both.

I used to think my childhood was extra dysfunctional. It is, but not so remarkable by the yardstick of other alcoholics and addicts. Every family has stuff. My ex-husband came from a proper South Carolinian family that pretended all was well and shoved problems under the table. My family had issues for all to see. I still am not sure which is healthier.

Perhaps we are all recovering from our childhoods. At least I don't know anyone who emerged unscathed.

And everyone has desire to fit in, especially during adolescence. I wanted to, desperately. I was a product of a biracial couple, who was forbidden by law to marry in our home state of Maryland.[1] My white father was an alcoholic who was arrested at our home, in front of the neighbors, for beating my mother. I did not know anyone else who had been arrested, especially a parent. I was humiliated and afraid.

My brother and I were also the only children of color in my all white suburban D.C. neighborhood, and two of the few children of a divorced couple in my parochial school. Since the Catholic Church at that time excommunicated divorcees, our father dropped off my brother and me at church every Sunday to attend mass alone, amid the large Irish Catholic families that surrounded us. There were girls from school who were forbidden to come to my house because my parents were divorced.

3

My paternal grandparents moved in with us after my mother left. I am unsure even today if my father kicked her out or she left because my father beat her. Somehow, my father had custody of my brother and me during weekdays. He probably was able to depict my mother as unstable; she once ran away with my brother and me for fear of losing us, and she had been seeking solace from her abusive husband in the arms of others. At least that's what I was told. I think racism played a role in my white father gaining custody of us. My father threatened to have my Filipina mother deported after their divorce. She swiftly got a job at an embassy to thwart his plan.

The Catholicism of my youth felt punitive. Fire and brimstone. But I have learned, post-50, to take what feeds me spiritually and disregard what I believe to be man-made mistakes. Maybe being a cafeteria Catholic is hypocritical to some, but it works for me.

Kids can be cruel to one another. I felt like a freak. I still remember an incident in third grade—ridiculous, I know—in which the pack leader of our class started the "freckle club" and I was the only one who had none. Denial of membership still smarts when I think about fragile eight-year-old Maria. Another vivid and hurtful memory is when a classmate told me I had "nigger lips." That derisive sentiment did not stop him from attempting shortly thereafter to jam his tongue in my mouth at the eighth-grade graduation party, much to my horror. I did not even know, at that point in my life, that anyone kissed like that.

I spent a great deal of my early life trying to assimilate. My mother was an immigrant from the Philippines. The "No Colored" signs on D.C. restaurant doors when she came here to pursue her master's degree in finance during the 1960s sometimes applied to her and sometimes did not. The prejudice in this country seems to have been directed more harshly at African Americans than other minorities, and her initial years in this country must have been confusing. She chose not to teach me her native language and most of her customs. She wanted me to be "American."

When my mother came to the United States, she planned never to return to the Philippines. As was common with many immigrants from lesser developed countries, she believed America was the land of opportunity. She believed the streets here were paved with gold.

My white father and brown mother married after a short courtship, and had me soon thereafter. My grandmother sent a series of nannies from the Philippines to care for me. My brother was born a year after me, and my Filipina grandmother came to stay for good.

My "Nana" was the strongest woman I have ever known. She also was a skilled entrepreneur. She birthed my mother in Manila during World War II. According to her account, hours after giving birth, she evacuated the hospital with her newborn to avoid a Japanese bombing assault. She went to her grave with a hatred for the Japanese because of the atrocities she witnessed during the war.

While on the island to which she and her small family were evacuated, she assessed that the food supply would not suffice, so she quickly gathered and purchased all the coconuts she could find. When food became scarce, she sold the coconuts at a large profit. I like to think that I inherited my resourceful nature from her.

Although I loved my Nana dearly, I was embarrassed by her carrying a parasol to shield her relatively light skin. During summer months, I did not mind tanning. As teens, my friends and I would try to tan, slicking our bodies with baby oil, unaware then of the sun's deleterious effect. My mother frequently would say to me, "Why are you letting yourself get so dark? You look like a farmhand!" I did not understand the colorism of her culture. Being lighter skinned was widely regarded by Asians to be of higher stature and closer to the ideal in beauty standards. I later learned that colorism was not uncommon among people of color.

My mother and grandmother had heavy accents. I laugh now, remembering funny things my mom would say, like "Stop driving so erratically," which came out sounding like, "Stop driving so erotically!" Or, "I am going to marry Mr. Beach, so you will have to call me Mrs. Beach," the surname being pronounced by her as "Bitch." But as a child, I cringed.

My mother married another white man, who had five children. The mother of those children walked away, so my mother helped my stepfather raise them. My family felt so much more complicated than other people's families. It got further complicated when my father married a much younger woman and together they had my half brother. All of this contributed to my feeling different from my peers.

Like most kids, I just wanted to fit in. In 1970s suburban Maryland, I wore Levi jeans and wished for my feet to grow faster so I could wear Chucks sneakers. I wore my hair for a while like Olympic medalist Dorothy Hamill. I became a teen and tortured my pin-straight hair into a semblance of the then-popular Farrah Fawcett hairdo. But I couldn't lighten my dark skin color.

One kid in my neighborhood taunted me with rice paddy jokes and slurs. I wanted to be tall, blond, thin, and white. Farrah Fawcett and Cheryl Tiegs were the most admired pinup gals of that era, which seemed to translate into the tall blondes being the most popular in my neighborhood as well. Sadly, it was not until my 20s that I began to embrace my cultural heritage and uniqueness.

Abuse is part of my story, as is rape. I was sexually abused when I was a child. I thought I was a freak and did not tell anyone about it until I was about to get married and worried about protecting my future children. I learned later, in therapy, that one in four girls will be sexually abused before they turn 18 years old.[2]

I coped by pretending these things never happened. But the wounds began leaking and eventually burst open. I entered a deep depression and was almost catatonic. Through therapy and medication, I got through it. I allowed other women to bear witness to my pain. We helped each other become not only survivors, but thrivers.

With no older siblings, and having parents who were fighting their own struggles, I tried to fit in. First it was through sports. Later, it was through drinking.

I spent a long time running away from my childhood. I sought refuge in books. I once read Emily Post's *Guide to Etiquette* cover to cover because I knew my family was different and wanted to know how to do things the "right" way.

I was a straight A student, which gave me something of which to be proud. At least getting good grades kept my mother off my back. And my maternal grandmother gave me money for every A on my report cards. My Filipina mother wanted me to become a doctor or a lawyer, which seemed to be the most respected occupations in her culture. Since I fainted at the sight of blood, I chose the law. I became a lawyer not because I loved the law; I wanted to please my mother and had no idea what I wanted to do with my life.

By-products of my particular childhood experiences included resourcefulness and the ability to compartmentalize, pretending certain dark things never happened. The former served me well in life; the latter caused a breakdown. I had a chameleon-like personality that allowed me to assimilate fairly easily. But the fear of being discovered to be a fraud haunted me, as did the double consciousness of moving through a white-dominated culture as a dark-skinned person.[3]

There are, of course, certain things from childhood all of us would benefit from retaining. The most important one may be the childlike sense of wonder about the world. The Toltec shaman and bestselling author don Miguel Ruiz reminds us of how free we were before the world changed us:

> The real you is still a little child who never grew up. Sometimes that little child comes out when you are having fun or playing, when you feel happy, when you are painting, or writing poetry, or playing the piano, or expressing yourself in some way. These are the happiest moments of your life—when the real you comes out, when you don't care about the past and you don't worry about the future. You are childlike.[4]

This ability to recapture that sense of presence and wonder may lead you to your 50 new things. My concerted effort to do so certainly led to some of mine.

· 2 ·

The Emptiness of Materialism and Trap of Perfectionism

I graduated from a well-regarded law school in the flush 1980s. Top-tier law school graduates were courted and wined and dined. At age 25, I was making almost six figures (adjusted for inflation, which was a great deal for someone my age).

I met my husband while in law school. His WASP-y grandmother, upon seeing my photo, asked if I could speak English. His family was anti-Catholic also. We married anyway. He is a good, ethical, smart man.

My husband and I each got high-paying jobs at large law firms in Washington, D.C. We bought a house downtown, and entertained and went out frequently. I scored a job as a political appointee in the Clinton administration and enjoyed the headiness of spending time at the White House and working on matters that constituted breaking news.

Five years after marrying, we had a baby and moved to a tony suburb. We joined a country club and a yacht club (though we owned no boat). I played a lot of tennis and hosted coffees and fund-raisers. We summered in Nantucket. I learned that some used "summer" as a verb.

In our all-white neighborhood, I was frequently mistaken for the nanny of my lighter-skinned children. People at the country club mistook me for a waitress there on several occasions. It was annoying, and I wrote a couple of books about those experiences.[1]

I hid behind designer items to try to make me feel better about myself. Perhaps if I wore expensive clothing and jewelry, people would like me better or respect me more, I thought. Maybe my BMW or Mercedes would confer extra status upon me. I have learned, unfortunately not earlier than at age 50, that anyone who would hold me in higher esteem because of my material things are not the people with whom I want to spend time. With age comes wisdom.

I cared too much about appearances—of my house, my kids, my husband, the food I served. . . . I relentlessly organized events in my neighborhood, at my children's schools, for charities and at my home. I had thousands of "friends," but failed to nurture the friendships that meant the most to me. My 40th birthday party began with an invitation list of 1,000 people, which I whittled down to 200, per my husband's reasonable request. My life at that time was exhausting.

Other than the unconditional love I had for my children, I felt fraudulent and empty.

Post-50, I no longer lust after material objects. I much prefer experiences over things. I learned that the thrill of obtaining a material item is fleeting and that, as Theodore Roosevelt once said, "Comparison is the thief of joy."[2] What I have is enough. I am enough.

I so often confused pleasure and excitement with happiness. Happiness, for me now, is more about contentment and serenity. They last much longer.

The trap of perfectionism was likely a contributing factor to the snap that took place the year my father died. His death forced me, in a way, to stop and look within and behind me. Not places I was comfortable visiting. Like a rubber band that was stretched beyond its strength allowed, I plummeted and then joined the sisterhood of the selective serotonin reuptake inhibitor (SSRI) takers.

The faithful say everything happens for a reason. Depression, in some quarters, is a closely held secret. I have learned that hidden depression can be fatal and that working through depression can sometimes serve as a gateway to clarity on many levels.

When my father died, I snapped. My social and other obligations came to a screeching halt. I felt as if I were floating above my life. My closest friend said I was a ghost of myself.

I am normally chatty and gregarious. I can talk for 20 miles of a marathon, and have done so three times. Something was seriously wrong with me. I went silent for months, and spent hours staring at the wall.

A therapist informed me that my depression was likely caused, at least in part, by unexpressed rage. I had assumed the depression stemmed from the sorrow of losing my father to cancer and the ugliness my stepmother caused while he was dying and as we planned his memorial service.

While on his cancer-stricken deathbed, my father shared information with me about my mother—things I had long suppressed and had no need to know on a conscious level, like her infidelity. It probably was an attempt to exonerate himself for how broken, drunk, and harsh he had been when I was a child. He died very shortly after telling me. I had no idea how to process the information.

Was the divorce my mother's fault? Or had she sought solace in the arms of another because my father was a violent alcoholic? Maybe it was a chicken/egg situation. I doubt I will ever know the truth.

I mourned for the innocent child I was, caught in the crosshairs of my parents' misery and actions. Children are fine observers but poor interpreters. What had I thought? How did my parents' issues affect me? How did they affect my now middle-aged brother, who I did my best to parent, though it was not my responsibility to do so?

According to the Anxiety and Depression Association of America (ADAA),[3] depression is one of the most common mental disorders in the United States. Approximately 15.7 million, or 6.7 percent, of American adults have experienced at least one major depressive episode. It is treatable, yet only about one-third of those who need it in our country seek treatment. Stigma regarding mental issues remains in our society. This is especially so for the older demographic that was raised with the mentality that one must pick themselves up and persevere at all times, and that a family's dirty laundry was not to be aired outside the home. But nontreatment can lead to suicide. I now know 10 people who have taken their own lives. I definitely thought about it and was convinced not to do it, at least for my children's sake.

I love my children fiercely and would do anything in my power to save them from harm. But my mind was so skewed that I thought my children would be better off without me. After I shared that sentiment at a 12-step meeting, a kindly stranger looked me in the eye and said, "Every child is worse off if their parent kills herself!" That was enough to stop me. In that moment, at least.

The taboo regarding depression and other mental illnesses needs to be eradicated. If you think you have depression, please get help from a medical professional. There are various levels of depression and many ways of treating it. Do not suffer alone. You are not alone.[4]

It surprises me how many people have no familiarity with clinical depression. Some of my friends and family members implored me to snap out of my depression and anxiety. I wish I could have. It was like being in a hole and not being able to extricate myself from the murky molasses-like muck holding me down. It feels otherworldly. My viewpoint was all out of whack, which is not surprising in retrospect, given that depression is a chemical imbalance in the brain.

On the other hand, there is a huge percentage of the population that takes medication for depression. According to National Public Radio, one in 10 Americans takes antidepressants.[5] The highest demographic of those getting antidepressant medication prescriptions is women in their 40s and 50s.[6] After I began speaking openly about my antidepressant medication use, women seemed to come out of the woodwork, sharing about their use of these sometimes lifesaving drugs.

Why middle-aged women? Perhaps men suffer in silence. Maybe they are socialized not to show emotion or weakness. In any event, it is my firm belief that by continuing to cultivate passions in life, midlife angst and even depression can be mitigated. Once my clinical depression was treated with medication, my horizons expanded exponentially.

The most commonly prescribed medications for depression are SSRIs, such as Zoloft, Prozac, and Lexapro. They ease depression by increasing levels of serotonin in the brain.

It was intensely frustrating to me, however, that those who wish to take medication to treat anxiety and depression often must try several medications before finding the one that is right for them. And most medications take several weeks before their efficacy can be experienced. It seems to me that modern medicine would have found a way to test our blood or brain waves to save us from this human test tube-like experimentation. But they have not.[7] I ended up trying five different medications before I felt relief from a medication with tolerable side effects.

I did not rely on finding a magic pill, however. I tried to exercise, engaged in talk therapy, and forced myself to get out of the house each day (though I spent a great deal of time staring at the walls). Forays to the grocery store took hours. It felt very difficult to choose items there. Too many choices stymied me.

I felt ridiculously anxious. My then-husband and best friend tried to help me calm my exaggerated fearfulness. There was a period when I implored my husband every morning not to leave for work. I simultaneously worried that my problems were too big for him to handle and that if he really knew what was going on inside my head, he would leave me. A few times, I even thought I heard voices. Inside the refrigerator. When alone, I would stay so still that I once saw a field mouse peek out from under the oven and look at me.

There is a generational resistance to mental health treatment. My parents' generation was mostly of the stiff upper lip sort. The potential for shame outweighed the potential for feeling better. Thank God this was not a factor for me, though I admit that I lost a few friends during the time I was severely depressed. Those who did not understand depression's effects kept their distance from me. I understand that people are resistant to things they do not understand, and that they would prefer to keep company with upbeat friends.

But when I got well, I remembered who stood by my side during the dark days and naturally gravitated toward them.

One of the medications I took made me zombielike. Another made me manic. The mania-inducing one was much preferred. Filled with long-lost energy, I sprang into action, starting numerous projects.

I also upped my alcohol intake. A lot. And the medication magnified the intoxicating effect of the alcohol. It was not a good mix.

I started buying cheap wine by the case and hiding the bottles around the house. My husband started noticing the empties, first in our recycling bin, then in our neighbor's. "Yes, such a coincidence that they drink the same wine. Big sale at the local store," I'd reply. He was skeptical, and started finding my alcohol stashes in various places in the house. Maybe I wanted to get caught. Maybe this was a cry for help.

I drank out of opaque plastic cups or other glasses that did not resemble wineglasses. Sometimes, I would bring roadies when I drove carpool from my children's schools. Bad mother. Lucky I didn't kill them. Or me. Or anyone else.

I knew I had a drinking problem in high school and college because I had so many blackouts. During one of these blackouts in high school, I was raped. I found out 20 years later that someone watched while this occurred. The observer told me himself.

I drunkenly lit my hair on fire once, by mistake, at a football game. I woke up in strange places, unsure of how I had gotten there. I favored Long Island Iced Teas because they got me obliterated the most quickly. Luckily, I mostly had friends who watched out for me, going to the effort of rescuing me from a bikers' place at the beach one summer when I had passed out there during my teenage years. I got myself into very dangerous situations while drunk, and could have died on several occasions.

My drinking subsided during pregnancy and early motherhood. My desire to be the kind of mother I had yearned for somehow overrode my compulsion to drink during those years.

It raged back with a vengeance when I came out of my depression. It fueled my mania. And then it didn't. It got me into loads of trouble. My husband gave me several chances to get sober. He really tried. He sent me to rehab. He came to family weekends there, and was understanding, to a point. Eventually, justifiably tired of my drunken escapades and disgusted by my terrible relapses between rehab stays, he told me not to return home.

• 3 •

A Living Problem

My 13-year-old son walked across the stage to accept an award at his highly regarded private school's eighth-grade graduation. I was not there. I was in rehab. I pictured the Chanel- and Burberry-clad, well-heeled parents discussing where the room parent was during this grand celebration. I imagined teachers asking my son where his normally omnipresent mother was and him responding, "Oh, she couldn't make it. She's in rehab." Ugh. I just tried not to think about it.

I never in a million years thought I would end up in rehab.

Recovery, at least, frees you from worrying about what others think about you. Once we addicts fully uncover our demons, we are able to search for our most authentic selves. Sharing openly about my sobriety enabled me to help numerous women who had been grappling alone with the disease of alcoholism and the attendant shame. I wrote an article for *Washingtonian* magazine that caused many of my picture-perfect friends and acquaintances to ask me to take them to their first 12-step meeting.[1] Before I started going to meetings, on several occasions, I sat outside in my car at a meeting site, afraid to go in. When I finally got the courage to enter a meeting, I found one of my oldest friends there. I had no idea he was in long-term recovery. Had I known, I may have asked him for help much earlier. He took me to meetings every day for my first weeks in recovery. He introduced me to many women in the program, including my sponsor. For that, I will be forever grateful and will strive to pay it forward.

I had preferred to run from my skeletons for the prior 40-plus years. They were safely tucked away. I believed no one in my former country club life would understand the darkness of my past. The "ladies who lunch," with whom I often shared company, could not possibly relate to my tortured childhood involving sexual abuse, police arresting my father for beating my mom, half brothers, step-siblings, racial slurs, and microaggressions. We were all so adept at making our lives appear so unblemished, so Tiffany-blue designer aubergine color-coordinated, so wrapped in mansion walls or, at least, picket fences. I overcompensated for my low sense of self-worth by attempting to over-function, people-please, organize and run as many events as possible in school, church, and neighborhood communities. My next-door neighbor jokingly called me the "mayor" of the town, and remarked that she gave my house as a landmark when telling people where she lived. My house was the frequent site of neighborhood welcome coffees, book clubs, fund-raisers, and dinner parties. My daughter and son attended prestigious private schools. My then-husband was an Ivy League–educated attorney, who had been well reared in Charleston, South Carolina. He provided well for our family. I gave up my law practice to attempt to create a modern Norman Rockwellian family life and to pretend that I belonged in the well-to-do WASP-y extended family and country clubs we joined.

At least my children had the childhood I had longed for. I had not screwed that up. I gave them everything I had wanted as a child—a mom who was home for them, involved in their schools and was the Girl Scout troop leader; tennis, golf, piano, dance, swimming, and sailing lessons; cotillion to learn social graces; fashionable clothes; travel; family dinners almost every night; availability to help with homework; and a parent who attended every sporting and school event.

In some ways, I tried too hard. When my children hit their teen years, they naturally stopped needing me so much and affirmatively tried to cut the apron strings, pushing away their over-involved mom. I went from knowing everyone in their circles to being given occasional scraps of information about their personal interactions outside our home. I was overeager to meet their friends and peppered them with inquiries that elicited the opposite of the intended effect.

I did not know how to let go of my children properly and to give them their needed space. I felt untethered, having put too many of my eggs in the motherhood basket. I did everything in my power to nurture my children, but failed to give my relationship with my husband the attention it deserved. I had let him slip pretty far down the totem-pole of my attention recipients. Our Westie dog arguably received more of me on a daily basis.

My depression following my father's death had turned me into a ghost of myself. Then, I began surreptitiously drinking by myself, until it became a two wine bottles a day habit. The antidepression medication I took magnified the effects of the alcohol.

The more I reflected on it, in some ways, the excessive drinking and attendant outrageous and self-sabotaging behavior may have been a backward cry for help. I recycled my cases of empty wine bottles, not just out of concern for Mother Earth. I probably wanted someone to notice them. The mounting pile of them. Empty, like I felt.

The demons would not stay away. I snapped and couldn't run anymore. My husband gave me an ultimatum and I went to 12-step meetings and then to rehab, one of five I checked into in 2012.

Each one taught me something different and had slightly different approaches. The first one, Caron Treatment Center in Wernersville, Pennsylvania, convinced me through medical studies and presentations that alcoholism is a disease, as diabetes is a disease, and that it has a strong genetic component.

My father and grandfather were both alcoholics. I would frequently arrive home during my teen years to find my father alone in a darkened living room, listening to Barbra Streisand on the record player and crying into his beer. He would look up and moan, "Angeline (my mother's name), why did you leave me?" I would respond, "I am not Angeline! I am your daughter!" as I ran up the stairs and locked myself into my bedroom.

My grandfather died of the disease of alcoholism. He was a proud colonel, who had served in World War II. His wife, my namesake, lived with us and suffered from Alzheimer's disease. His martini glass seemed rarely empty. I can still picture the amber bottles with the four roses label. The numbing liquid corroded his liver and took his life.

Caron showed us studies that the brains of alcoholics metabolize alcohol differently from those of nonalcoholics. As a lifelong Catholic, hatched during the days of pre–Vatican II brimstone, I had thought alcoholism was a matter of free will and a moral failing. I now know it is a cunning and baffling disease. It ruined my marriage and other relationships. I lied to my doctor about my excessive alcohol intake when she presented medical tests evidencing my liver's destruction.

My rehab group therapist practiced a tough love approach. My first day, I attempted to defend a patient who was being yelled at by the therapist for violating a rule. He turned on me and shouted, "Maria! Take off your fucking nurse's hat and get the hell out of this room!" Stunned, I pinched my bottom cheeks together to keep from crying—a tactic a rehab friend had suggested that actually works. The therapist had my number. He knew I would rather focus on anyone else's problems but my own. Deflection would no longer prevent introspection by this alcoholic.

My counselor at Caron thought I needed trauma counseling and recommended I go to The Ranch outside Nashville for intensive treatment for post-traumatic stress disorder (PTSD) for some sexual assault and abuse issues

I had avoided for many years. I decided it was about time. I never wanted to leave my family for rehab again. I cried every day in rehab. One fellow patient nicknamed me "the human water sprinkler."

My greatest flow of tears followed the Sunday chapel services, which elicited a roller coaster of emotions. I listened to families giving testimony about how their loved ones were saved by rehab. I saw fellow alcoholics and drug addicts break down in despair and drag themselves back up. I saw musicians sing or play instruments, performing for the first time sober. Witnessing this was so moving to me that I later started open mic nights at my recovery club.

I sought out the priest, Father Bill, after one of the services. I asked if he would hear my confession. He replied, with his hand touching my head, "You are forgiven for everything you did while in the clutches of this disease. Go out and sin no more." I felt healing in this encounter.

From the PTSD rehab, I learned that not dealing with one's issues is like holding a beach ball under water. One can do it, but it takes a tremendous amount of energy. And whatever it is that one is not dealing with unwittingly pops up in unexpected ways. This explained a lot of the sideways behavior in which I had engaged in my life. Learning to forgive ourselves is a necessary part of recovery.

Those in recovery often beat ourselves up over our mistakes. My sponsor encouraged me to question my interior dialogue when railing against myself. Sometimes it helps for me to ask if I would allow someone to speak to my children or a close friend in this way. Then I am more often able to choose compassion for myself.

I benefited from equine therapy at this PTSD rehab. I had been fearful of horses. I learned that horses are ultrasensitive to the emotions of those around them. They tend not to cooperate, for example, if they sense fear from the one giving them commands. We cared for the horses and learned how to build mutual trust. Overcoming fear gave me confidence I needed as I rebuilt my life.

The biggest lesson I learned at this rehab was the necessity of asking for help with addiction. The counselors engaged us in a powerful exercise. We were blindfolded and put into a maze. We were told that there was only one way out of the maze. I was nearly the last one out. As I heard others making their way out, my determination to find the exit doubled. The counselors shared with me later that it was often those, like me, with advanced degrees who were the last out of the maze. They thought they could think their way out of the maze. But the only way out of this maze was to ask for help—not something I will ever easily forget after this frustrating, yet compelling reminder.

Another difficult lesson for me was physically letting go by jumping off a high cliff (while harnessed). I am afraid of heights. I cried atop that cliff but moved through the fear, while putting my fate in God's hands. We were told that courage is moving through fear. Powerful exercise. I am still afraid of heights, though.

The counselors made us say daily affirmations while looking in a mirror. We were required to say three positive things about ourselves before every group session. After saying each one, the rest of the group would robustly respond, "Yes you are!" In the beginning, I thought saying affirmations was a silly ritual. Over time, I came to believe my affirmations and truly felt a boost in confidence when I said them. I now have affirmations posted on my mirror at home and they do serve as personal buttresses. A few of my favorites:

"I am patient and serene, for I have the rest of my life in which to grow."

"Every experience I have in life (even unpleasant ones) contributes to my learning and growth."

"I am a worthwhile and lovable human being."

"I have a Higher Power who loves me unconditionally."

"I create my reality."

"I am a child of God."

Everyone I met in rehab was, like me, broken. Some of their stories made me involuntarily recoil. I did not know our brand of desperation could lead someone to chug mouthwash or vanilla extract for the temporary escapism its alcohol content provided. I met a young woman who, while under the influence of hallucinogenic drugs, had attempted to peel off all of the skin on her arms, and had the gruesome scars to show for it. I got to know a middle-aged woman who downed laundry bleach because she could no longer stand her pain.

When a heavily made-up 20-year-old with red dyed locks and four-inch heels, showing too much leg and cleavage joined our therapy group, I winced listening to her harrowing stories of living in a crack house and turning tricks for sick middle-aged men—the straight, white, married men asking for the most deviant of services—just to get her hands on another rock of cocaine. One client paid her to beat him with her fists. Others paid her to violate them with strap-on instruments or to watch her do twisted things with other people.

I had no idea simply by looking at her that she may have been a prostitute. One of the hard-core addicts laughed at my surprise and joked, "Maria! Do you live under a rock? I took one look at her and said, 'please, God, may there be an ATM here!'" (so that he could get cash to avail himself of sexual services from her). A sick joke.

I became protective of this woman, especially since she was close to my daughter's age. She was passionate about animals and hoped to work in a zoo someday. She even claimed that the rats in her former crack house did not bother her. I looked up programs during the 20-minute Internet allotment I was given occasionally, to give her a few leads. Her father wanted her to come back and work in the family's business. She had her misgivings. "I can make a thousand bucks an hour with one old white guy who just wants me to beat him up," the Lolita shared. "I don't really want to sit in an office." I never found out what happened to her, but continue to pray that she found a better life.

We both shared a friendship with a gorgeous, former Ford model with a crystal meth addiction. She was bashful and doelike. I visited her after our rehab stay to meet her baby, who seemed to give her a reason for living a clean life. A year later, she died from an overdose.

Another friend at this rehab had abused his liver so badly due to drinking that it visibly protruded from his abdomen. He almost had to carry it sometimes, supporting it with his arms. His wife pleaded with him to stop killing himself. He could not.

One of my rehab roommates told me she had been placed there for "violence against others." I looked at her and asked, "Are you going to hurt me?" She slowly looked me up and down before responding, "No." I did not sleep well the one night we shared a room together.

Another roommate committed suicide a few years after leaving the rehab. It is unlikely that I will ever know why she took her life. I do know that there is more to sobriety than not taking a drink or a drug, and that my battle to achieve emotional sobriety will take even longer than it took for me to stop seeking solace in a bottle. I pray that I never will stop working my 12-step program. There are many more layers of this onion to peel.

I saw several well-known celebrities during my rehab stays. Like me, they put their pants on one leg at a time. And, like me, they were working on self-discovery and healing. Rehab is a shared journey of raw humanity, and no one is above or below another on the journey.

Out of respect for their privacy, I shall not reveal by name the famous guests I met in rehab. They are, however, household names and people of immense talent. I helped one internationally successful musician work on a song, though I doubt she ever used it commercially. I do smile, though, when I see her in the media, and silently cheer her on in her recovery.

The smorgasbord of people in rehab and in the recovery rooms never ceases to amaze me. And that we share so truthfully on a human level without judgment in rehab and recovery rooms is something I have not experienced elsewhere.

I had not fully surrendered and relapsed after the first two rehab stays. I took dangerous drugs in an effort to hurt myself. I do not even enjoy drugs. I have seen these drugs kill others, but when a fellow sufferer gave them to me, I did not decline the offer. At that time, I was considering running my car into trees I passed, or jumping off bridges to end my pain. One of the benefits of not anaesthetizing with alcohol is that I can fully feel my feelings; this benefit also can be tough to bear, especially in early sobriety before learning how to use the tools of the program.

I was filled with self-loathing and could not believe how low I had fallen. Part of me did not truly believe I was an alcoholic or addict. Part of me believed I could tackle my alcohol abuse without examining the pain that has plagued me throughout my life. Part of me believed I could control myself and my life, and that prior lapses were moral failings. Part of me did not believe I deserved the life I had.

There is something called the "pink cloud" that many recovering alcoholics and addicts experience. It is a floating, heady feeling when one becomes newly sober. It is temporary, however, and has led many an alcoholic to let their guard down against this cunning, powerful and baffling foe.

I became complacent, at a time that I should have remained vigilant. My disease took me to horrifying places. So I returned to rehabs three through five.

I got kicked out of rehab number three. I was angry at myself and struggling with shame over the additional mistakes I had made. I fought with the counselors, demanding reasons for their excessive rules. The rules were in place in an attempt to keep us safe, but also to force us to give up control. Surrendering to a power greater than ourselves, whom I choose to call God, is an integral part of recovery. The approach at this particular rehab, however, was exactly opposite of what would have been effective for me at this point. I was in a chaotic, rebellious phase and their punitive measures only fueled my desire to act out. The more they prohibited me from doing something, the more attractive that something appeared to me. I had regressed into my former teenage behavior. It disgusts me now to think about how I behaved then.

One of my character defects had been the inclination to do the opposite of what a given person wanted me to do, if I felt he or she were trying to control me. This was often to my detriment. I berated myself for all the things I should or should not have done in my past. But I have learned to stop "shoulding" all over myself. I look for the lesson and focus on the precious present.

Getting kicked out turned out to be somewhat of a blessing. I moved on to rehab number four, which led me to much self-discovery and healing. I spent most of my time there uncovering and examining the root causes for my sick behavior. The counselors there were excellent, and they treated a panoply of issues. I stopped fighting so hard.

Rehab number five was my finishing school. It was a transitional program for women. It provided periods of freedom in which we could put the tools we learned there to work. I had no car, but learned to love bike riding again. I got myself to recovery meetings "off-campus." I learned self-regulation, using cognitive behavioral therapy.

I also learned during my stay at number five that I was no longer welcome at my house and that my husband of almost 25 years wanted a divorce. I was stunned. I thought he would take me back after I returned to sane behavior. But the irreparable damage had been done, and he needed to protect his heart.

My alcoholism and reckless behavior was linked inextricably to my PTSD, my feeling of being less-than, my inability to deal with life on life's terms. It was a form of flight. It crept into my affairs like ivy, slowly invading every aspect. I am convinced, as were some of my rehab therapists, that I would be dead now if I had not gotten help.

I came to rehab and the 12-step rooms to quit drinking, but the Twelve Steps I learned there ended up changing my life. They provided a road map I'd always yearned for, a guide for living.[2] They were crafted carefully in a specific order and have saved many people from dying from this disease of alcoholism or other addictions:

- Step One: We admitted that we were powerless over alcohol and that our lives had become unmanageable.
- Step Two: Came to believe that a Power greater than ourselves could restore us to sanity.
- Step Three: Made a decision to turn our will and our lives over to the care of God *as we understood Him.*
- Step Four: Made a searching and fearless moral inventory of ourselves.
- Step Five: Admitted to God, to ourselves, and to another human being the exact nature of our wrongs.
- Step Six: Were entirely ready to have God remove all these defects of character.
- Step Seven: Humbly asked Him to remove our shortcomings.
- Step Eight: Made a list of all persons we had harmed, and became willing to make amends to them all.
- Step Nine: Made direct amends to such people whenever possible, except when to do so would injure them or others.
- Step Ten: Continued to take personal inventory and when we were wrong promptly admitted it.
- Step Eleven: Sought through prayer and meditation to improve our conscious contact with God *as we understood Him*, praying only for knowledge of His will for us and the power to carry that out.

• Step Twelve: Having had a spiritual awakening as the result of these steps, we tried to carry this message to alcoholics, and to practice these principles in all our affairs.[3]

The Steps are brilliantly designed to appeal to agnostics, atheists, and those of any religious beliefs. While the word God is used in the Steps, the literature makes clear that what is being referred to is an individual's Higher Power, whom many choose to call God. Some people I know choose to call the power they find in the fellowship to be their Higher Power. No one in the program must believe in God, though most come to believe in something bigger than themselves. The only requirement for membership in the 12-step recovery program is a desire to stop drinking.[4]

The 12-step program is rich with pithy slogans that seemed silly at first, but have saved many an alcoholic, including me, as they became ingrained in one's psyche. Slogans I see in almost every recovery meeting room include: "Think, think, think," "Easy Does It," "One Day at a Time," "First Things First," "Let go and let God," and "But for the Grace of God." The sayings were easy to dismiss as platitudes until I surrendered and allowed them to start working in my life. Among the many gems I learned from showing up, day after day, in the rooms:

★Acceptance is the answer to all of my problems. Acceptance is not tantamount to resignation. It is saying "yes" to what is. As the most resonant part of the "Big Book" in my 12-step recovery program says:

> acceptance is the answer to *all* my problems today. When I am disturbed, it is because I find some person, place, thing, or situation—some fact of my life—unacceptable to me, and I can find no serenity until I accept that person, place or thing, or situation as being exactly the way it is supposed to be at this moment. Nothing, absolutely nothing, happens in God's world by mistake. Until I could accept my alcoholism, I could not stay sober; unless I accept life completely on life's terms, I cannot be happy. I need to concentrate not so much on what needs to be changed in the world as on what needs to be changed in me and my attitudes.[5]

We thereby adopt a central tenet of Buddhism: We must either accept the truth or suffer.

Sometimes I find myself saying the Serenity Prayer[6] ten times a day. Freedom from fear is more important than freedom from want. I had spent many hours in my former life worrying about things that seem insignificant now, and certainly outside of my control. Now, I have an effective check on that practice. I ask myself, can I control this? If the answer is no, I accept it. Worrying deprives me of the joy of living in the present. I have learned to Let

Go and Let God, aka, Let Go or Be Dragged. Life has improved tremendously for me since I began trying to wear life like a loose garment.

There are many things over which we have no control. But there are a great many that we can control. The most life-altering for me is controlling my attitude. I used to be greatly affected, for example, by how others felt about me and behaved toward me. If someone says something bitter or mean-spirited to me, I now can pause and not allow it to affect me negatively. I can respond with compassion or disinterest, or not at all. I do not have to react. No one can make me feel a certain way. I, alone, can choose my feelings and response.

Traffic and poor drivers impeding my way used to irritate me a great deal. I choose now, however, not to let such potential irritants anger me. I choose instead to focus on my breathing, make a mental gratitude list (remembering, for instance, that I am fortunate enough to have a car and the ability to drive it) or listen to a book on tape. I subscribe to audible.com and always have books available in the queue. I have CDs in my car of recovery speakers I admire, that help keep me on the beam and pass the time on long drives. I protect my serenity as much as possible. It took me five decades to find it.

Anger is a luxury not afforded to alcoholics. The deleterious effects of anger are illuminated in the Dalai Lama's writings.[7] Anger destroys our peace of mind. It can cause ulcers and high blood pressure. It makes us ugly inside and out, as our facial and other muscles tense. Our feelings of anger do nothing to the object of our negative sentiment. The Buddha says that "holding onto anger is like drinking poison and expecting the other person to die." In a similar vein, my anger used to spur me to drink *at* my problems or the person I perceived to be causing me problems. How crazy is that logic?

Similar effects can occur from worry. "Who of you by worrying can add a single hour to his life span?" is a biblical admonition that is especially important to me at this stage in my life, when there are more years behind me than in front of me.[8] So when I feel worry bubbling up, I first ask myself if I can control anything about which I am anxious. If not, I need to let go of it, because it will help no one, and will affect the quality of my present life negatively. For example, even though I would like to keep my children in a protective bubble, I cannot. I must have faith that now, as adults, they will make the right choices. They must live their own lives and make their own mistakes. I am learning to accept that I can no longer helicopter-parent them.

Sometimes, for a particularly vexing issue, I go through the act of writing it down and putting it in something I call my God Box. The act of physically putting something away for God to handle underscores how the problem is out of my control. It is, for me, a symbolic surrender, a laying down of my sword.

★*Bless them; change me.* When I am pointing my finger at someone, there are four other fingers pointing back at me. In recovery, I have learned to pray for difficult people.

I now pray for the people who have hurt me deeply, taken advantage of me, or betrayed me. It does not mean I have to keep company with them, of course. It helps alleviate any negative feelings I have toward them by picturing them as hurt children, or adults continuing to carry childhood scars. We never fully know what is going on in another person's life and what challenge or sadness they face. So I choose to practice compassion for myself and for others by not reacting to the behavior of others, but rather responding with love.

We learn in recovery that it is important to clean up our side of the street. We must acknowledge our part in any issues and make amends for our mistakes, in order to heal from our "dis-ease." Now I can also see more clearly the role I played in any perceived wrongs done unto me and quickly do what I can to fix whatever problem to which I have contributed.

I can live my amends to my children by staying sober and doing the next right thing. I cannot change the past, but I can write a new ending. I can look for the lessons in what happened. As the poet Rumi says, "the wound is the place where the light enters you."[9]

I went to my father's and grandfather's graves at Arlington National Cemetery to apologize to them. My loud sobbing startled some tourists who had come to pay their respects to other veterans. But saying I was sorry to both of these men was cathartic for me.

I attempted to make amends to all I had harmed in the past. With one exception, they appreciated my gestures and apologies. The one former friend who declined my invitation to meet with me to receive my amends is no longer in my life. But I am able to let any sorrow involving her go now.

★*Pleasure and happiness are not the same thing.* Pleasure is fleeting. Happiness or serenity is of longer duration. It sometimes is the ability to live peacefully with the inevitable discomfort that comes our way. It is a feeling of contentment and the knowledge that everything is as it should be. It is not yearning for things one does not have, but relishing what one does have.

I chased pleasure in my youth. I fed off of thrills.

What I seek now is a sense of calm well-being. I get that most readily via meditation, especially coupled with being near water.

I have learned how to have fun without alcohol. I thought, when I became sober, that life without the social lubricant of alcohol could not possibly be as fun. But it is. In fact, it is better.

Part of recovery involves fellowship. I have made deep friendships in my recovery groups and we frequently socialize. There are sober softball leagues. One of my rehabs has offices in several cities and organizes outings to sports events, concerts, and other fun opportunities. My recovery club sponsors parties, cookouts, dances, dinners, and open mic nights. And we each can remember the next day what happened at these events.

When the student is ready, the teacher will come. The amount of denial most alcoholics and addicts like me practiced is astounding. The acronym "DE-NIAL" reminds me that, as a drunk, I "Don't Even Notice I Am Lying." For many of us, the pattern of lying or denial during active alcoholism became so ingrained that we even lied for no reason at times. Recovery reveals to us such patterns. We become aware and then ready to change.

No one in the recovery rooms cares what your profession is or how much or little wealth you may have. I have heard people there say, "We don't care if you came from Yale or jail; if you want sobriety, you are welcome." No one comes to the rooms because their lives are going swimmingly well. We are all just "bozos on the bus." We surrendered to the program and will of our Higher Power because we had hit our own personal bottoms. We were sick and tired of being sick and tired. We know that continuing on the addictive path we were on would lead to death, jail, or institutions. We became ready for a better way of living.

I have learned great wisdom from homeless sober fellows, as well as from learned doctors in the recovery rooms. I used to surround myself with beautiful, financially successful people. Now I surround myself with people who help me be the best version of myself that I can be. There is something for me to learn from all of those trudging the road to happy destiny. There is something for me to learn from pain and difficult people. The famous poet Rumi[10] says that each guest in our lives is sent to teach us something, and that we can learn if we greet such opportunities with an open heart.

The opposite of addiction is connection. We alcoholics cannot recover by ourselves. It is nothing short of a miracle that so many have gained relief from the disease of alcoholism and other addictions by being in rooms with fellow sufferers. There is power in the "We."

Those in the program who do not believe in God sometimes made their recovery group their "Higher Power." Human community most certainly can act as a protective wall. I personally believe that the recovery group is one manifestation of my Higher Power, whom I choose to call God, and that these worldwide recovery programs wisely chose to appeal to all people, including those who do not believe in God.

Some of my nonalcoholic friends have said, "You are cured now, so you can have a drink with us." They do not understand that recovery is a lifelong process. I have met many alcoholics with decades of sobriety who relapse when they let their guard down and become complacent with their program. We addicts must remain vigilant because the disease is a cunning foe. Our culture is infused with alcohol references. Happy hours abound. "Let's meet for drinks" is a common refrain. Jokes about wine making things better emblazon cards, plaques, towels, and signs. Drinking is the norm in American culture.

We call those who can control their drinking "normies." We marvel that normies can walk away from a drink without finishing it. If I start drinking again, I am likely to take a bottle from behind the bar and gulp it down in a bathroom stall. Or worse.

I plan to go to recovery meetings for the rest of my life. Meetings keep me centered, aware, and safe from my disease. I instantly connect with people in the meetings and feel welcome in any room I visit. And part of giving back is being there for other alcoholics.

Twelve-step meetings exist in most countries and all over the United States. They are online and available by phone. The program and meetings are not secret, but are not publicized. They often take place in churches. I chose a regular home group based on the meetings in which I found I could relate more closely to the attendants. Women's meetings remain my favorite.

Women in the program said to me, "We will love you until you can love yourself." I believed it. That feeling propelled me forward. When I went through my painful divorce, the words of my sponsor were at the forefront of my mind: "You will be protected." And I was, by these wonderful sobriety sisters.

We celebrate each other's successes and share our pain. Pain shared is halved. Joy shared is doubled. In fact, I initially was shocked and even annoyed by all the laughter I heard in the rooms. "How can these people be laughing when I am so miserable?" I wondered. Now I understand and can find the humor in life—even in the tough parts of it.

Sometimes, "If I don't throw it up, I'll drink it down" (i.e., if I do not share something weighing on me, I am one step closer to relapsing on alcohol). I scrutinize every decision to evaluate whether it brings me closer to or further from recovery. We take care not to isolate and watch to ensure none of our sobriety sisters is so doing.

★We are responsible for our own happiness. We will experience the consequences of our own self-love or self-hate. I believe more now in the power of attraction and manifesting our own abundance.

There are so many pearls of wisdom to be gleaned from those in sobriety, and I continue to learn something new every day. I had to change so much about myself. I have to stay away from the people, places, and things that are triggers to me. "Don't go into a 'barbershop' unless you want a 'haircut,'" my recovery sponsor warned.

The winds of life continue to affect me, but now I have tools to deal with them without seeking temporary refuge in the bottle. I learned that I did not have a drinking problem; I had a living problem.

No one can *make* me happy or sad. I choose my own responses to life. I experience my emotions and no longer stuff them away. If I am upset, I allow the emotion to wash over me like a wave. Then I let it go. I take solace in the belief that if I do not experience the depths, I cannot experience the heights.

It is important to acknowledge that change can be scary for those around you. Sobriety demands that we alcoholics change a great deal about ourselves. If we return to the conditions that led us to drink, we are likely to continue to imbibe. We are embarking in recovery on a new way of living.

My atheist sister-in-law felt threatened when her husband got into 12-step recovery because it felt cultish and full of God-talk. My heavy drinker friends did not like the mirror of sobriety held up to them. My ex-husband felt resentful of all of the time I was spending with my sponsor in my early days of sobriety. Some relationships died natural deaths after I chose a new path for myself. The instant kinship I felt with fellow people in recovery was more comfortable for me than my previously exciting, whirling social life. My previous world shattered as I became more fully whole.

I believe that the miracles of the 12-step program are the best-kept secret in the world. Everyone would benefit by following the Twelve Steps. It could accurately be called the 12 steps to being a good human.

Twelve-step meetings provide spiritual showers for me. Every meeting I attend is like putting spiritual capital in the bank. They keep me centered and committed to recovery. Newcomers remind me where I was and how far I have come, and long-timers inspire me with their experience, strength, and hope. Recovery conferences typically draw the most gifted speakers among us, and often end with hundreds or even thousands of people holding hands around the convention center room as we recite the Serenity Prayer together.

The Promises come true to those who stay in the program:

1. If we are painstaking about this phase of our development, we will be amazed before we are halfway through.
2. We are going to know a new freedom and a new happiness.
3. We will not regret the past nor wish to shut the door on it.
4. We will comprehend the word serenity and we will know peace.
5. No matter how far down the scale we have gone, we will see how our experience can benefit others.
6. That feeling of uselessness and self-pity will disappear.
7. We will lose interest in selfish things and gain interest in our fellows.
8. Self-seeking will slip away.
9. Our whole attitude and outlook upon life will change.

10. Fear of people and of economic insecurity will leave us.
11. We will intuitively know how to handle situations which used to baffle us.
12. We will suddenly realize that God is doing for us what we could not do for ourselves. Are these extravagant promises? We think not. They are being fulfilled among us—sometimes quickly, sometimes slowly. They will always materialize if we work for them.[11]

• *4* •

Dry Drunk Grad School

"*W*ould you rather be right or happy?" Provocative question for which I did not have a clear answer before I got sober.

I was not alone. Until we alcoholics learn to follow the Twelve Steps, many of us are what we term "dry drunks." We may be physically sober (i.e., not drinking alcohol), but not emotionally sober. Another 12-step group that was started to help families and friends of alcoholics also helps the alcoholic—and anyone else, really—with relationships and emotional sobriety.

I came to the rooms of 12-step recovery to quit drinking, but the experience ended up changing my life. It provided a road map I had always yearned for, a guide for living. Once the compulsion to drink was lifted, there were relationships to address.

I had not heard the term "codependent" prior to entering rehab. Once there, however, I was made aware that the term fit my emotional behavior.[1] For example, my happiness was largely dependent on the happiness of my children. I would die for them. But they each have their own Higher Power. And it's not me. I have to allow them to learn from their mistakes and not try to shield them from such learning opportunities.

I had to learn to take a few steps back and to develop healthy boundaries. I learned that I am only responsible for my own well-being, and not that of others. Each person has the right to choose if and when to change anything in his or her life. I was under the delusion that I could control my teenagers. I learned to listen more, instead of trying always to fix things, which was a sea change for me. I offered advice only when asked, which led my children to ask more.

Parenting most clearly challenges the lessons of what I can and cannot control. Our children are put in our charge, but not forever. My job was to help equip them to be adults on their own. When I see traces of myself in my children, I start to worry that they could face some of the challenges I had, or make some of the same painful mistakes. But I cannot force them to do anything, or cease from doing anything. I must allow them to live their own lives, even if I do not agree with some of their choices. As a recovering overprotective mother, that is very difficult for me to do. I need the support of my 12-step program to not become mired in worry and to refrain from my enabling tendencies. I love my children unconditionally and would save them every ounce of pain if I could, but I cannot. I have learned to love and appreciate the moments of grace I experience with them. I know they love me; they know I love them and am here for them. I pray every day that they find their way and are relatively unscathed when they arrive.

The 12-step program for people with alcoholics in their lives has been referred to as "grad school for alcoholics." In it, I have learned how to have healthy relationships. Twelve-step programs for codependents and adult children of alcoholics also helped. Really any 12-step program would help this alcoholic. I once wandered into a 12-step meeting for food addicts because I felt at risk and needed some centering and support at that very moment. The attendees welcomed me with open arms. And the steps were the same. I could just substitute the word "alcohol" for food and then could identify with all that was discussed.

One of the central themes in this program is detaching with love. We learn the Three C's: We did not *cause* it, we cannot *control* it, and we cannot *cure* it. We cannot fix another person, but we can work on ourselves. We can learn not to react. We can make choices that are good for our own well-being. There is no person we can change except for ourselves. The acronym DETACH comes to mean Don't Even Think About Changing Him/Her.

I actively practice nonattachment. I try not to be attached to outcomes or ways of achieving outcomes. I try not to be attached in an unhealthy way to my loved ones. I try to see others as equals, not elevated in a way that gives them power over me and feeds my false sense of unworthiness.

Another way of detaching with love is "holding a place" for someone. I think of my children and send them love and good energy. I cannot direct my children's lives, but I can observe with interest. One of my recovery teachers likened this practice to being seated in the first row of a play. You are engaged, but you do not get on stage and interfere with the production. This metaphor made sense to me and has saved me from meddling—as much as I used to meddle.

When I finally realized just how little I had control over, those things on which I spent a lot of emotional bandwidth lost their control over me. I regained the time I had spent future-tripping over things that may or may not happen. I learned to live in the present and to stop fighting my Higher Power's will.

As Holocaust survivor Viktor Frankl wrote in *Man's Search for Meaning*, "Everything can be taken from a man but one thing: the last of the human freedoms—to choose one's attitude in any given set of circumstances, to choose one's own way."[2] We always can choose our response to a given happening. I read Dr. Frankl's powerful words while in rehab. I took them to heart several years later, when I was ready. Sometimes it is a matter now of my asking myself if I would rather be right or happy before I respond.

Nonattachment does not require me to relinquish my dreams. It means that I must remain open to learning about myself, and responding rather than reacting. In this way, I can become a more complete and serene version of myself.

A helpful 12-step tool I use every day is to frequently ask myself, before speaking, "Does it need to be said; does it need to be said by me; and does it need to be said now?" This little exercise has saved me much conflict.

Though I always have leaned toward being a glass-half-full, optimistic person, another important tool I use is gratitude lists, especially with regard to my relationships. The lens through which I choose to see my loved ones has changed. I now focus on the good in various people, rather than amplifying the bad. In my current romantic relationship, my beau and I text each other every day one thing we appreciate about the other person. The item can be profound or prosaic. I am fond of how his eyes crinkle in the corners when he smiles. I am inspired by how he helps so many men in recovery.

And the traits I most appreciate in people have changed. Kindness tops my list. I surround myself with people who help me to be the best version of myself that I can be. I avoid psychic vampires and toxic people. I stay away from people, places, and things that are triggering for me.

Another change: I no longer believe in soul mates. I was sure I could live a Hallmark-card life, and tried my best to mold myself and my family life into my perceived ideal. I realize now the folly of my fantasy, which probably was a reaction to how dysfunctional my childhood had been, exacerbated by the illusion of Facebook post–worthy lives around me. I now believe we each have the capacity to be our own soul mates, and that no person and no relationship can be perfect. We are all perfectly imperfect.

Twelve-step programs are not without issues, of course. Any man-made institution has them. Many participants in recovery programs suffer from dual diagnoses or mental illness. It is not uncommon for those in recovery to substitute one addiction for another. I was warned to avoid those who may try to "13th step" me (i.e., prey on newcomers when we are at our most vulnerable). In fact, participants are counseled not to engage in any romantic relationships during their first year of recovery.

Also, like so many others in recovery, I started smoking when I stopped drinking. In rehab, the smoking areas were social outings of sorts. Smoking was one of the few vices we were allowed in rehab. I had absolutely no business smoking. I watched my father die a gruesome death from lung cancer following years of smoking. I realized that when I was upset, I gravitated toward self-harm. Lingering self-hatred, I suppose.

I quit smoking about a year ago. A friend told me he quit because he wanted to maximize the chances he would be alive to walk his daughter down the aisle at her wedding. I, too, want to be there at my children's milestone celebrations. I want to be a part of my grandchildren's lives, if I am lucky enough to have them. My sugar addiction may be the next habit I will work on eradicating from my life. Moderation has not been my strong suit.

We are asked in these recovery programs to put principles over personalities. This is sometimes a challenge for me. I have to refrain from judgment and taking other people's inventories. We learn that when we figuratively point our fingers at someone else, there are four other fingers pointing back at us. What we abhor in other people is frequently a reflection of what we dislike about ourselves in some respect, or a form of insecurity.

We in recovery often cannot control our first thought. But we learn to control our second thought and, of course, our actions. We learn to practice the pause before speaking or responding. We call it "practicing restraint of pen and tongue." I often call my sponsor before taking an action I am unsure of and she always provides wise counsel. She helps me learn self-care and appropriate boundaries.

Boundaries. Something I had not been very good at creating or respecting. I have been abused—physically, sexually, and emotionally—so many times that I have wondered if I have "abuse me" psychically emblazoned on my forehead. I devalued and gave away pieces of myself.

I learned, through therapy, that because I had been violated sexually at a critical developmental juncture early in my life, I had trouble maintaining boundaries. Many who are sexually abused become either sexually anorexic or promiscuous. There were times in my life that I used my body as a weapon, or as a means to feel that I had power. I would f*** them before they could f*** me. Eroticized rage. As other suffering women I have met have attempted, I tried to fill the hole in my soul with men. I also tried to seek affirmation via the attention of others. Pathetic, misguided thinking. I now try to fill the hole in my soul with myself and, more importantly, with my Higher Power. I have begun to repair my battered soul.

Perhaps the worst boundary-violating incident occurred in a hospital on Nantucket the summer my father died. I was experiencing suicidal ideation and my then-husband took me to the hospital there. Shortly after arriving, I became paranoid that my children would be taken away from me if I were shown to be mentally disturbed. So I demanded to be released. They told me I would have to be cleared by a mental health practitioner before they would let me go and that there was only one psychiatrist available on the entire island.

He arrived and I told him how my father's death unleashed a Pandora's box of horribles. I told him of the sexual abuse I had endured as a child, the rape when I was in high school, and the pain I had hidden for years. He gazed at me with lecherous eyes. I froze. He said, "Hugging therapy works." I remained corpselike as he ran his hands over my flimsy hospital gown-covered body. It was like a bear was attacking me and I was playing dead. So he lost interest, I think. I am not sure. I was no longer there.

I did not tell anyone about what happened until about five years later. At the time of the incident, I was afraid no one would believe me, and my priority was getting out of that hospital and retaining my children. When I returned to Nantucket, I shared about what happened during a recovery meeting. A woman there who was married to a police officer helped me find out about the abuser. It turns out that he was fired for molesting children at the facility where he worked and had left the island. I regret not reporting the abuse when it happened.

I finally allowed other women to bear witness to my pain and to all that happened. I am still not ready to face my abusers. But sharing with other women helped me heal. It is as though a scab has formed over the wounds. I now can share about my experience without tears.

What I continue to work on, however, is approval-seeking and emotional hangovers when I get reprimanded or rejected in some way. This, I have learned, is a common problem for those who have been abused. We measured our self-worth via the reactions of others. Oh, how much time I have wasted seeking approval. I am well on the road to recovering from this character defect.

Alcoholism and relationship recovery also provided me with a healthier perspective.[3] I realized that many of my problems were "first-world" problems. I knew I would have a roof over my head and food to eat on any given day, though plenty of fellow alcoholics lost even these comforts. Concentrated gratitude changed a great deal for me. I do not indulge myself on the "pity pot" anymore. I strive to pass on what I have learned to help others.

So now that you know a great deal of my dirt, let's talk about you. Hopefully, your life has not been filled with as many traumas and mistakes as mine.

Regardless, we women today are blessed with the ability to chapter our lives and to grow as we age. The fact that we are middle-aged does not mean we must remain stagnant or wither. In fact, those of us who stay active or try to learn new things live longer, healthier, and happier lives.

Fifty is a good reckoning point for most of us. Age 50 can be an igniting point to the most invigorating chapter yet. As our familial responsibilities become less all-consuming and hopefully before true physical decline sets in, this is a way for women to reclaim their authenticity and discover what truly makes them happy.

I remember years ago being simultaneously horrified and intrigued by Pulitzer Prize–winning novelist Anne Tyler's *Ladder of Years*.[4] In this book, the protagonist, a middle-aged wife and mother of three, simply walks away from her life and starts anew. She tires of the monotony of her everyday life and the way she is taken for granted by those around her, for whom she is becoming less necessary. The description of middle-aged angst, and the abrupt and extreme way Tyler's character attempts to escape it, beguiled and haunted me. What would I do differently if I could walk away from everything? I am not suggesting you abandon your present life and responsibilities. But even fantasizing about the prospect can be instructive.

How many of us know people this age, including ourselves, who have middle-aged blues? Well, help yourself—and your friends—design a blueprint for turning midlife into the most exciting and fulfilling chapter yet. Take the time to reevaluate and recalibrate before it is too late to secure a life well lived. Cut out the things that no longer serve you and explore what does or might. It's your life, and it's up to you what you do with it.

II

INTRODUCING MY LIST OF 50

*M*y life circumstances demanded a new beginning. I was newly sober, newly single, and a recent empty-nester, crossing over the half-century mark in my life. I needed new goals and direction. On my 50th birthday, I decided to embark on trying 50 new things, many of which took me out of my comfort zone. Each activity or change taught me something new. From hiking in the Himalayas to getting my motorcycle license to choosing to surround myself only with people who bring out the good in me, I sought to drink fully from the cup of life. My wide-ranging list may not be your cup of tea. But I can almost guarantee that my list will spark creative lists in those of you who are ready to make this chapter of your lives your best one yet.

Some of the items on my list of 50 involved little commitment. Some altered the tenor and possibly the course of my life. The point for me was an awareness of my mortality creeping closer, a desire to make the most of the time remaining and a mission to make this world a better place because I was here.

Perhaps a bit by necessity—I divorced and did not ask for alimony because I felt so guilty for drinking my way out of my marriage—I decided that I did not need any more material things. I wanted essentials and experiences only. So I saved money and looked for new ways of making money to attain my goals.

I sold things on eBay and Craigslist, consigned clothing and accessories I no longer needed, furnished my home with secondhand items, and embraced the minimalist movement. You might be surprised at what sells on online sites. There was a local news story on how many bids a seller got for a pencil. You never know what item of yours that you no longer want or need is desirable to someone else.

I got several part-time jobs as a contract lawyer, worked at author events for an independent bookstore, and did freelance writing and editing. I even had an errand service as a side business for a while, and set up an Etsy shop online to sell some paintings I had done. I rented my home out on weekends via Airbnb and Vacation Rental by Owner (VRBO) to make some quick cash for traveling.

Then I did the soul-searching. What made me happy? Aside from my children, I was hard-pressed to say. I felt as if I had lost myself along the way. Pursuing 50 new things was part of my quest to find out who I was at my core and what made me happy.

The definition of happiness is debatable. In my youth, it meant pleasure and excitement. Those things can contribute to happiness, but I was looking for something less fleeting. At 50, happiness means contentment, serenity, peace. With some spice mixed in.

Some people call after-50 the "third third" of our lives. We are not dead yet! Numerous studies hail the benefits of remaining active and continuing to grow. I strive to learn something new every day. We all should.

Your list of 50 may be radically different from mine. These are the things that spoke to me, and not every one of them will appeal to you. And not every single thing I tried is something I care to repeat, like acupuncture, for instance.

The list includes activities and changes big and small. It is arranged thematically into the following groupings: (1) travel and adventure; (2) learning and teaching; (3) social activities; (4) physical challenges and well-being; (5) spiritual endeavors; (6) thrill-seeking ventures; and (7) lifestyle changes. I encourage you to try items from each category, to add variety, and to stimulate your mental, spiritual, and physical muscles. Make some changes. Realign your priorities. Shed what no longer serves you. Stay vibrant. We do not need to fade as we age.

My list is designed to inspire you, as it has with so many women with whom I have shared it. Challenge yourself, before life throws its next curve ball. You are worth it.

• 5 •

Travel and Adventure

My kids were away at school. My marriage was over. I had saved some money to get away. I assured myself that I was not running away, but running toward something—lessons, rich experiences, and finding out more about myself and the world at large. Travel—even to a new town a few miles away—always has led to mind expansion for me. It enriches; it increases empathy, tolerance, and understanding. It can make us even more grateful to have been born in the United States in situations of opportunity.

And I know how to travel on a shoestring budget. If you do not, there are plenty of books and websites dedicated to budget travel.[1] To be the most successful at saving money while traveling, I need to have time to research discounts and deals. My research always has paid off. Flexibility to travel at nonpeak times or on short notice helps lower costs as well. And if one volunteers, the nonprofit organization often will pay for a significant percentage, if not all, of your costs.[2]

I have several female friends who have designed their careers and work so that it can be done from anywhere. As I write these words, my friend Chezzie Brungraber is hiking in the Swiss mountains with her baby and husband and working when they have Wi-Fi™. She arranged her work life so that she could work very hard on her business for part of the year and then travel for the rest of it. My friend Desiree Garcia travels around the country with her mobile healing massage services. In the last year, I have seen her—and enjoyed her massage services—at two yoga festivals. Her children are now grown and she can support herself with her work wherever she wants to be.[3] Several former colleagues worked very long hours over a necessary period until they could retire early and see the world. This kind of life is possible with appropriate planning.

I greatly admire W. Kamau Bell's chosen adventures. On his CNN documentary television show, *United Shades of America*, Bell explores communities that could not be more different from where he lives.[4] He has visited Ku Klux Klan meetings, prisons for the most violent criminals, Native American reservations, and other unusual destinations. Through these forays, he and his viewers gain understanding about viewpoints that may differ vastly from our own.

While I was lucky to be able to travel to distant places, the lessons afforded by going to new places can be gleaned from near travel as well. A walk through an unfamiliar neighborhood, park, or city can bring excitement, stimulation, and increased understanding.

There are many more places in the world I want to see before I die. The beaches of Vietnam, the island of Mauritius, the Badlands of the western United States, the Burning Man annual village in the California desert, and the Canary Islands are among them. When compiling my 50 After 50 list, I had to start somewhere, and I made a large dent in my lifelong bucket list the year I turned 50. I used to research extensively before I visited somewhere new. Now, I build in more time to allow experiences to unfold. My daughter recently saw a sign in a Cambodian hostel that said something like, "Travelers see what they see; tourists see what they came to see."

The point is to experience somewhere you have not before been and to take a break from your day-to-day life, to refresh and possibly reset it. Getaways do not have to be far away or expensive. Staycations can provide needed respite, and can be done in novel ways.[5] TripAdvisor can help you find things nearby and provides other travelers' reviews about any place that piques your interest.[6] Airbnb has started connecting travelers with experience opportunities to try out in various areas, like guided tours, classes, games, tastings, photo shoots, picnics, shopping with professional stylists, and hikes.[7] Let me know what you find.

1. Volunteer Vacation

> *The meaning of life is to find your gift.*
> *The purpose of life is to give it away.*

—Pablo Picasso

I needed space from my old life. I yearned to "get outta Dodge." I was not seeking a geographical cure to my woes necessarily, but something more like a sabbatical—some distance, so that I could assess where I had been and where I wanted to go from here.

I went almost exactly to the other side of the world. I had wanted to experience some adventure and to do some good in the world. I settled on Nepal.

The trip started on an auspicious note. I got bumped up to first class, which had never before happened to me. I have never wanted to spend my money on added comfort while in transit, but now I know why people choose to do that.

The stars aligned when I befriended a woman who was the first Nepali woman to become a U.S. marine. Her relatives put me in contact with some schools in Nepal. One was in Kathmandu and one was in the poorest region of Nepal—Karnali. I volunteered at both of the schools. By comparison, the school in Kathmandu was posh. The students wore uniforms and there were books in the classrooms and inspirational posters on the walls. Some of the students were orphans. Most spoke English and looked well cared for. Those without parents lived in a nearby dormitory. A friend from home had adopted three of the young women and was paying for their expenses.

The second school was high in the mountains. We took a small plane to the only nearby town of Jumla. There was no security to speak of when passing through the airport. I was surprised to find a rooster sticking his head out of a box next to me. I was even more surprised when a tiny man stepped on board, saw that all seats were taken, then jumped on my guide's lap for the trip. My guide was happy to oblige. Seat belts were optional.

I had come to Karnali with school supplies. We caught a jeep up a mud path riddled with large holes for a short portion of the journey. I left that harrowing ride in tears after teetering precariously along cliff edges. Because there was no road leading to the school, however, two of the parents from the village who came to welcome me carried the boxes of school supplies atop their heads. They nimbly navigated the miles of rocks and rugged uphill terrain that took me eight hours to hike up. No one would have described my hiking technique as nimble. . . .

I doubt I will ever forget the reception I received from the people in Karnali. They had never met a Westerner. A band of six drummers came down the path to meet me when I arrived at the school. The entire village came to the school to welcome me. I received dozens of wreaths of flowers, popcorn, and bundles of greens. I could barely see over my colorful adornments. Many speeches were made. A holy man blessed me with a crimson tika upon my forehead. It was surreal, humbling, and a bit embarrassing. I was no celebrity, after all. Yet they treated me as if I possessed some sort of magical power. Several mothers asked me to touch their infants.

The 120 students aged three to 14 lined up with palms together as if in prayer. We bowed to each other individually, saying "Namaste." Despite their tattered clothing and open sores, they were achingly beautiful.

The school in Karnali lacked electricity, heat, and running water. Some of the children had no shoes, despite the snow on the ground. The floors of the classrooms were simply dirt, and the children sat on the floor for their lessons. I saw no books. Most of the teachers were volunteers. Some of the villagers said that the Nepali government had forgotten about that remote part of Nepal. It was hard to disagree.

I was struck by how happy the students were, despite their lack of creature comforts. I visited several of their homes for ginger tea, most of which afforded little respite from the harsh weather. One of the villagers put me up for the weeks I was there. Although neither my hosts nor I could speak each other's language, we managed to communicate. We spent all of our free time huddled around the kitchen stove. There was no electricity or running water in their simple stone house. The guest of honor bed I was given consisted of a table covered by some blankets. The frozen outhouse was a place I tried to avoid, especially at night. Visits to the outhouse sometimes were complicated by whiteout snow conditions and the need to put one's boots back on since no shoes are worn indoors. I stopped drinking fluids after 5:00 p.m.

The hosts insisted that we eat before they ate. They were reluctant to allow me to help with any home chores. After several weeks, the woman of the house allowed me to grind corn into cornmeal in their primitive grinder, and to milk the cows and feed the chickens.

I was made starkly aware of the many things I take for granted. Like mattresses. Heat. Socks. Napkins. Utensils. Toilet paper. Toothpaste. The majority of Himalayan people do not own toothbrushes or know much about oral care, I was told. I tried not to let the lack of sanitation upend me, though traveling here is certainly not for those accustomed to a posh lifestyle—or a lifestyle based on any sort of schedule. For example, a bus arrives at the closest town (a nine-hour hike away) once each day, but no one knows what time it will come on a given day. I learned how to have fewer expectations there.

I am forever changed by this experience. I kept the thin layer of privileged guilt and self-consciousness at bay, so that I could maintain a positive attitude while working and living there.

The villagers dreamed of building a library for the children of Karnali. One of the village's residents walked across the country to Kathmandu, found a job washing dishes, put himself through college, and found a way to the United States, where he got a job as a translator. The villagers rightly regarded him as a hero. He and I met on several occasions in the United States and were able to raise enough funds to build a children's library in Karnali.

I collected loads of books for the library after it was built. Government tariffs and complications prevented the books from being shipped and carried to the library. Someday, however, I will return to see this happy but forlorn village.

I made a small corner of the world a bit better because I was there. You can, too. And I am sure you do not have to go far to do that. Look online for a volunteer vacation,[8] or in your community for a charitable endeavor, if you do not want to create one of your own. The point is that helping others helps us get out of ourselves. We gain perspective. We increase our self-esteem by doing esteemable acts.

I originally had hoped to enter the Peace Corps, after learning that retirees make up a large percent of its volunteer population, but my life circumstances do not allow for that at the present time. But with this one trip, my heart swelled with pride and a renewed sense of purpose.

What can you do to make this world a better place?

2. A Very Long Hike

I took a walk in the woods
and came out taller than the trees.

—Henry David Thoreau

Trekking in the Himalayas had been on my bucket list for years. I was not exactly searching for James Hilton's Shangri-La, though the thought of finding it held appeal. Shangri-La is a fictional place described in the 1933 novel *Lost Horizon*.[9] Shangri-La is described as a mystical, harmonious valley. It has become synonymous with any earthly paradise, particularly a mythical Himalayan utopia—a permanently happy land, isolated from the outside world.

In some ways, I found a version of Shangri-La. The terrain was largely unspoiled. We frequently found ourselves above the clouds. Sometimes herds of sheep and goats slowed us. We stopped to admire the white monkeys who gazed at us from tree limbs. I marveled at the rhododendron forests, with the tallest of that species I had ever seen. There were no roads, save for a few muddy paths here and there near the base of the mountains. The people I encountered were shut off from the rest of the world and rarely came down from their high abodes.

The people seemed content with so little. Children played with sticks and improvised toys. Anything not growing naturally in the Himalayas had to be carried many miles upward, so the Himalayan dwellers made do with less. Maybe that was the key to their contentment. They accepted their lives as they were. The experience gave me a dose of humility, perspective, and gratitude for being born in the United States, with attendant privileges (like clean bathrooms and modern toilets).

There was no luxury travel for this intrepid soul. I was back to my 20-something backpacking style. I actually brought my weathered L. L. Bean backpack from a two-month trip I took with a friend after taking the bar exam in 1988.

I did not find the mythical utopia. Even the "easiest" treks are not for the faint of heart. At times I felt as if I were carrying an anvil as I climbed in the higher elevations. But the payoff of witnessing a sunrise at 3,210 meters atop Poon Hill was one of my life's highlights.

A small crowd gathered at Poon Hill to see the sunrise. It was glorious. All conversation ceased the moment the sun breached the horizon. Even the most jaded among us was momentarily without words.

The planet's highest peaks are in the Himalayas. I had traveled to India and China in my 20s, but had never made it to Nepal, so I opted for a five-day trek on the Annapurna Circuit in north central Nepal. Annapurna is a Sanskrit name that has been translated by some to mean the "universal kitchen-goddess," and "the mother who feeds." How fitting for me, I thought. I planned to volunteer in Nepal after the trek, so I wanted a trek on the shorter side. Plus, I was out of shape.

My Sherpa guide was a trim, affable man whose English was spotty. That did not matter, except for the fact that I barely understood anything he said and thus never really knew our schedule. When he was ready to leave our electricity-free but affordable prayer flag–laden guest houses, I would gamely follow him.

The trek became somewhat of a series of silent walking meditations, which were difficult for this loquacious, recovering people-pleaser. I used to joke with my running group that I could talk for 20 miles (during our marathon training days), and then someone else would have to take on the task for the remainder of the run. And I proved I could, in fact, fill the air with 20 miles' worth of conversation on several occasions.

My ex-husband used to call me the "U.N. Rep" because I could talk to anyone and frequently approached strangers asking them if they needed help or photos taken.

I wanted to learn how to be a better listener. Quieting my mind and voice were things that allowed me to become better aware of what my Higher Power's will for me may be, something I was becoming more interested in than where my own stubborn and sometimes misguided will had brought me.

The people I encountered along the trek underscored my lack of endurance skills. There were no roads in that part of the world. Everything had to be lugged up the mountain. Elderly men and women with deeply etched wrinkled skin carried unfathomable amounts of things on their backs and heads. At one point, I asked an ancient-looking woman if I could try picking up her bundle. I could not even budge it. She cackled in laughter at my feeble attempts.

At the end of the trek, I felt exhausted, but cleansed in some way. My arthritic knees were taped up with duct tape toward the end of the journey. Atop and surrounded by the world's highest peaks, I reawakened my sense of wonder. The natural grandeur of the landscape made me gasp several times. It was cold and the trees glimmered from the snow that settled upon their limbs. The clouds dramatically shifted, darkened, and lightened from one moment to the next. I felt the presence of my Higher Power when I stared at the stunning beauty around me. I learned to just be on the journey without lamenting the past or future-tripping about what would happen next. I let go of expectations and gained perspective on my life. My divorce brought me sorrow, but I felt equipped to deal with the next chapter. Tears of gratitude filled my eyes. Renewal had begun.

Hiking in nature anywhere can be healing. Our country's national parks provide picturesque, accessible venues. I know several women who have hiked the Appalachian trail by themselves. One celebrated her 50th birthday with this feat. Author Cheryl Strayed captured the essence of her healing solo journey along the famous West Coast trail in her bestselling memoir, *Wild: From Lost to Found on the Pacific Coast Trail*.[10] I believe we all can heal by spending some alone time with Mother Nature.

3. Solo Safari

> *Nature is the art of God.*
>
> —Sir Thomas Browne

The lion was so close, I could see its fine whiskers move. My guide had no weapon and we were in an open-air vehicle. The lion looked regal and fierce. He looked satisfied, as if he had recently had a big meal, I told myself.

It was exciting, beautiful, and educational to be out in the wild, at the mercy of the majestic creatures whose habitat we visited. Animals emerged unexpectedly, and my senses were on high alert. There was an air of danger about, and I imagined predators sizing me up as we meandered around the wild terrain.

I wanted to take a photographic safari. Being in nature feeds me, and I find animals to be fascinating. Even observing my dog reminds me to stretch before physical activity. Nature can be a potent instructor.

I looked online, read reviews, and booked one on the low end of the pricing scale. It was a bit of a gamble, in that I did not know who else would be in the group. I had some fear, as well, about traveling alone as a woman. A small woman. I am not even five feet tall. But I am fairly feisty!

I lucked out. I found a reasonably priced safari to Kruger National Park, one of the largest of South Africa's game reserves. It is about the size of Israel or Wales.

There were two couples on the trip, one of whom was on their honeymoon. The other was from England and very jolly. I was the only solo traveler, but did not feel uncomfortable about that. Our guide was a grizzled old Afrikaner with a mischievous sense of humor. He was a big flirt, but harmless. He counseled us not to "donate" ourselves to the ferocious Cape buffalo we encountered, and jokingly tried to get me to stay in South Africa and be his companion.

I did a lot of research to find the lowest airfare and safari accommodations. After my time in Nepal, I was fine without many creature comforts.

The scenery and wildlife we saw were breathtaking. Witnessing the circle of life and survival of the fittest was perspective altering for me. I felt tiny. I felt amazed. I reveled in the wonders of nature in a way I seldom did in my adult life before this chapter.

I learned about the history of South Africa while on this safari, and could observe en route the remnants of the Apartheid era. Even in the bush, the white Afrikaners appeared to have the better jobs. The culture is an amalgam of Dutch, British, and tribal influences. It is financially more stable than most of the other countries on the continent, which inspired some xenophobia when outsiders tried to take South African jobs. Tourism plays a large role in the South African economy.

I stretched myself by going on an adventure on the other side of the world with people I knew nothing about. I could hear wild animals roaring around me at night, reminding me of nature's pecking order. I left with a greater understanding of one of the world's newest democracies and of African wildlife, which is so different from that indigenous to our continent. The adventure fed my spirit.

Of course one does not have to go around the world to experience adventure and stretch oneself. The theater of natural beauty can be found in many, many places you have never been. One of my friends takes daily walks along the Potomac River, marveling and posting about the never-ending discoveries of flora, fauna, and insect life she comes across. Another volunteers at a girls' camp each summer to get her dose of outdoor adventure. I have explored trails and parks with my dog that are close to my home, but make me feel far away from my usual environs.

Being outside and close to the earth can feed your spirit. Go. Now.

4. I'll Take Manhattan

> *Cut off as I am, it is inevitable that I should sometimes feel like a shadow walking in a shadowy world. When this happens I ask to be taken to New York City. Always I return home weary but I have the comforting certainty that mankind is real flesh and I myself am not a dream.*
>
> —Helen Keller

It is a life regret of mine that I never lived in bustling, captivating New York City. It is a city that never sleeps, filled with culture and excitement, where one can find whatever they want, 24 hours a day. I visit often, taking a $20 to $30 bus from the D.C. area and staying with a dear friend from high school, who lives in a rent-controlled walk-up on the Upper East Side.

It feels as if I have walked almost all of Manhattan via my trips over time. The island is fewer than 23 square miles, and I have spent a multitude of hours meandering along its grid. I ran the New York Marathon through the five boroughs when I was younger. There are so many distinct New York neighborhoods, each with their own special flavors and ethos. Some New Yorkers have told me they rarely leave a 10-block radius of where they live because they have all they need there.

Walking, for me, is the best way to get to know a place. Architectural details are more noticeable, and encounters with local people add color and understanding about a place's vibe.

There are many free walking tours offered in New York. You can find them online.[11] I availed myself of a free walking tour highlighting the city's graffiti as art and social commentary. I have a completely new appreciation for the artistic graffiti that mysteriously blooms on New York City's surfaces. Most of it is placed illegally. Serious graffiti artists are well known, and sometimes commissioned. There is a famous graffiti work by the artist Banksy at 79th and Broadway that I doubt I would have noticed had it not been for my tour guide.

Some graffiti artists enjoy "bombing" the city with their work. Some create "brandalized" art, or branded but not necessarily permitted. "Yarn-bombing," whereby artists create pieces made of yarn interwoven into fences, is another graffiti method I came to know while on this tour. The tour underscored my belief that art does not have to be expensive to be good.

On one of my walks, I crossed the Brooklyn Bridge. It was beautiful. I explored the part of Brooklyn by the water and then figured out how to ferry back to Manhattan for a few bucks. Brooklyn has undergone a renaissance and is a hot spot for young people and artists now. Definitely check it out if you are near that part of the country. People have told me that there are less expensive Airbnb accommodations in Brooklyn if you want to visit New York City overnight.

I also have availed myself of the bike rental stations that have popped up around Manhattan. I often beat the traffic by biking somewhere. Biking in Manhattan is not for the faint of heart, however. Ultra-crazy drivers, especially taxis, have come uncomfortably close to my two wheels. There are more and more bike lanes, which helps cyclists gain a bit more safety and room. My

New Yorker friends think I am out of my mind to ride a bike on these mean city streets. I like it.

New York is unlike anywhere else I have visited. There is always something to see or do, and many events are free.[12] I Google free events in New York before I visit and invariably find concerts, tours, festivals, and other activities that do not cost anything. I particularly enjoy the free concerts and Shakespeare productions in Central Park in the summer. On any given summer day, a walk through Central Park has yielded an entertaining surprise.

The most quoted and astute prose ever written about New York is by E. B. White in his essay, "Here is New York":[13]

> A poem compresses much in a small space and adds music, thus heightening its meaning. The city is like poetry; it compresses all life, all races and breeds, into a small island and adds music and the accompaniment of internal engines. The island of Manhattan is without any doubt the greatest human concentrate on earth, the poem whose magic is comprehensible to millions of permanent residents but whose full meaning will always remain elusive. At the feet of the tallest and plushiest offices lie the crummiest slums. The genteel mysteries housed in the Riverside Church are only a few blocks from the voodoo charms of Harlem. The merchant princes, riding to Wall Street in their limousines down the East River Drive, pass within a few hundred yards of the gypsy kings; but the princes do not know they are passing kings, and the kings are not up yet anyway—they live a more leisurely life than the princes and get drunk more consistently.

White notes in this essay the curious ability of New York to "bestow the gift of loneliness and the gift of privacy" to any person who "desires such queer prizes." That may be true, but it also exudes an electricity found nowhere else and appeals to my taste for possibility. And I sometimes relish the anonymity the city affords.

Pick a new place to learn about—on foot. It could be the town next to yours, or even the neighborhood that borders yours. Note what you discover that you would not have noticed while in a vehicle. I am interested to know what you find.

5. Traveling Shoes

Travel is fatal to narrow-mindedness.

—Mark Twain

While walking around by myself in Ubud, Indonesia, I came upon the town's cremation ceremony. It was not macabre in the least. It was a cacophony of music, chanting, pungent smells, and abundant offerings as the families bade adieu to the loved ones who had died over the past five years. It was fascinating to witness the rituals surrounding death in a country on the other side of the world, even when a half-dead chicken fell off an elaborate offering tower and unceremoniously plopped onto my foot.

I endeavor to go off the beaten path to be a student of the world. Travel is a mind-expanding opportunity for me, and I have learned how to travel on a low budget. I realize that my preferred style of travel is not for everyone. Once, when backpacking around Asia, my traveling companion lasted two days with me in China before ditching me for Club Med in Bali. She did not want to take public transportation. The Chinese—at least in 1988 Beijing— had public workers whose job it was to physically push as many people as possible into the buses. There seemed to be no appreciation of personal space.

My travels in this chapter of my life have included the Grand Canyon, Cape Town, Johannesburg, Nashville, Nepal, Gettysburg, Venice Beach, Montreal, Indonesia, the Philippines, Cape Cod, the Adirondacks, Munich, Doha, Chicago, Boston, and the Northeast Kingdom. Airbnb has increased affordable accommodation options in almost every venue.

All trips have enhanced my life in a different way. I try to hit a 12-step meeting every place I go, and I am lucky to have a boyfriend who likes to do the same. The people I have met along the way taught me various things, and I have learned not to judge a book by its cover.

I also have used travel as a means to learn more about my cultural heritage. My mother treated my children to a trip to the country of her youth— the Philippines—after my daughter graduated from college, and invited me to accompany them. I had only been to the Philippines once before, 30 years ago, as a gift for graduating from law school. It was a much different experience this time around. I possessed more context, cultural pride, and life experience at this juncture. I appreciated more of the nuances I observed.

The Philippines are an amalgam of Spanish, Malay, and American influences. It is unlike other Asian nations because of the colonial remnants. The joie de vivre and vibrancy of its people are infectious. Smiles and laughter come easily in this culture, as does singing. We were greeted and sent off with songs at a resort we visited. Karaoke and singing competition shows are popular there. Highly decorated, sometimes garish, Jeepneys are a common form of transportation. The Manila traffic, however, is not something I care to experience again any time soon.

It is also a country of great financial disparity. There appears to be not much of a middle class. We stayed in Manila with family friends who live in a lovely, large house, in a guarded walled community, with a staff of domestic help and drivers. Certain things that we take for granted in the United States, however, are lacking in their grand home. Because the price of electricity is very high, central air conditioning and clothes dryers are a luxury that is too dear for most. What is not expensive, however, is labor. Employment opportunities are such that a great deal of income in the Philippines comes from relatives who go off to work in the cities or other countries and send money home to their families. Remittances account for more than one-tenth of the gross domestic product of the Philippines.[14] The country's biggest export has become overseas Filipino workers. While a financial salve, the effect on separated families is quite deleterious. Witnessing this and being made more aware of how much of the world suffers to make ends meet is a sobering experience that helps me not take for granted the many blessings in my life.

I strive to see how the locals live and to experience a venue like a local when I travel. The way someone travels can reveal a great deal about a person. I parted company with one travel companion after I observed some "Ugly American" tendencies in his foreign travel behavior, such as assuming that everyone who sounded American was American when many times they were Canadian. Or expecting certain modern amenities in third world countries. Or simply speaking very loudly in a way that disturbs those around us.

Other world citizens, especially from Europe and Australia, do vacationing well. Americans typically take two weeks of vacation. Months off are not uncommon for European holidays.

I am encouraged to see the practice of sabbaticals taking hold in some parts of our country. Extended time away from the daily grind elevates our thinking and well-being. Any time away from daily routine is good for us, both for relaxation and reflection.

Sometimes, when I cannot get away physically, I read good work by travel writers. This practice is even more enjoyable while soaking in a warm tub or lying in a hammock. Author Peter Mayle has transported me to Provence with several of his books. Beryl Markham's *West with the Night* infused me with bravery for solo travel and a desire for more adventure.[15] In the mood for a wild road trip? Pick up Jack Kerouac's *On the Road*[16] for some explosive ideas. Enthusiasts of train travel might enjoy Paul Theroux's *The Great Railway Bazaar*,[17] recounting a journey across Europe, Asia, and the Middle East. A book like *Diners, Drive-ins and Dives*[18] may inspire you to plan your next U.S. venture. Someday, I plan to tour the United States in a recreational vehicle. Hopefully, I can finance that trip with some travel writing pieces. The world can be our oyster. There is so much more of it that I want to discover. Road trip, anyone?

6. Appreciating What's in My Own Backyard

The more one does and sees and feels, the more one is able to do, and the more genuine may be one's appreciation of fundamental things like home, and love, and understanding companionship.

—Amelia Earhart

I was born in Washington, D.C., and have lived in the D.C. area for most of my life. Our country's capital is filled with national treasures and unique opportunities. I realized in my fifth decade, however, that there were many D.C. venues, like museums and embassies, I had never seen. Maybe it is because there is such a wealth of such places here, that I had grown complacent that I would eventually get to them all.

It is easy to take for granted the natural and man-made wonders that grace our environs. One step I took to remedy this was to join a women's group that regularly visited embassies. They did the leg work and I went along for the ride. This group of mostly middle-aged women wanted to learn more about the world, and found a way to get embassy personnel to give us insight. Some embassies include a sampling of their traditional dishes when we visit.

The embassies also open their doors to the public on various Embassy Walk days. I took my daughter's Girl Scout troop to see some embassies years ago. The women's group gave us a more intimate and detailed view of the embassy and the country represented.

I also took a Segway tour around the Washington monuments and museums. I will admit that it took having an out-of-town guest visit to move me to do this thing I have wanted to try for a long time.

Riding on a Segway felt like floating on a hoverboard. Because they are electric, they make no sound. They are easy to control by using foot pressure—press on the balls of your feet, and the Segway goes faster; press on your heels and it slows and stops. We were given a lesson before setting out, and it felt very comfortable. I even learned a few historical tidbits that I did not know, such as that President Taft was the only U.S. president who also served as Chief Justice of the U.S. Supreme Court, and that the U.S. Capitol dome is made of cast iron.

Most of the museums in our nation's capital are free. The spectacular National Museum of African American History and Culture recently opened and is impossible to absorb in one visit. Most museums have changing special exhibitions, so there is always something new to see.

What have you not seen in your locality? The Internet, with travel sites such as TripAdvisor, makes it so much easier for us to discover and enjoy the banquet of delights around us. We are no longer in our dress rehearsal days. Life is happening right now. Get out and about before it is too late.

7. Food, Glorious Food

> *He was a bold man that first ate an oyster.*
>
> —Jonathan Swift

Food, for me, is one of life's greatest pleasures. I have a friend from law school who once said she wished there was a pill she could take every day instead of having to eat to stay alive. I was so startled by that notion that I remember the comment 30 years later.

I have another friend, Trisha de Borchgrave, who is a columnist on current affairs. She also is a talented artist and her intricate paintings of food reveal a deep respect for the natural fruits of our world. One of my favorites, a portrayal of leeks and garlic cloves, adorns my kitchen wall. Trisha's passion for a healthy-eating lifestyle is eloquently expressed:

> The refreshing fruits of that morning; instant energy from the banana's B6, magnesium and potassium; the blueberries, apple and kiwi enriching your brain and digestive system. Yet another step away from the storm, away from dementia, arthritis and heart failure.
>
> These foods are your real allies, guiding your moods and energy levels and providing the core of not only how you feel but who you are. Like a parent with your best interests at *heart*, these nutrients are on your side, they love *you*, working to maximise your potential, and your inner serenity, instead of leaving you to obsess about what not to eat.[19]

Her recent art show in Mallorca was called "Eat Food," of which she said:

> Fruit and vegetables are our guardian angels, always there to provide us with health; they are quiet but powerful reminders of why this planet is unique, and all our life within it. Our relationship to them—growing, nurturing and embracing them in our diet—is what truly connects us to the history of life and Mother Earth, to the continuity of our existence, from thousands of years ago to this very moment in time.

When Trisha lived nearby, meals with her were unhurried, delicious affairs, spiked with wide-ranging, thought-provoking, and witty conversations. In true European style (Trisha was raised on Mallorca), dinners went on for hours. America's busy lifestyle seems rarely to support such gatherings. But how delightful it is when we can slow down and savor an intimate meal with friends and family.

I always have considered cooking for other people an expression of caring for them. When someone in my circle of friends had a baby, we would do dinner showers for them, whereby we would each take a day for the month following the birth to drop off a dinner. At this stage, our practice is more often used when a friend is gravely ill or incapacitated in some way. When a friend loses a family member, arriving with food to help console, or at least to relieve someone of having to prepare meals, is customary. At this point in my life, I would rather bypass anything store-bought and gift someone with a homemade food item as an expression of my fondness for the recipient.

Sharing a meal with another is a bonding experience, as is cooking together. My daughter and I are trying to get my mother to teach us how she makes Filipino lumpia. It is a time-consuming process to make these delectable egg rolls, but it is part of our cultural heritage.

Now that I am cooking only for myself or a friend or two, I am able to indulge my love of food in a different way than when I was cooking nightly meals for my family. The availability of recipes online has opened a whole new avenue of dishes to try. Sometimes, if I happen to have an ingredient in my refrigerator that I want to use up, I look up recipes containing that ingredient and challenge myself to use the item in a new way.

I particularly like trying new foods and ethnic food. It is like a gastronomic travel interlude for me. Vibrant saffron coloring my rice can mentally transport me to a trip to India I once took. The smell of adobo and lechon make me think of my mother and Filipino relatives. Fresh salmon conjures up dinners with my Seattle friends. Coconut milk and sugarcane bring back a trek in northern Thailand. Beignets make me remember JazzFest in New Orleans.

When I travel, trying the local cuisine is a must, even if it looks unappetizing. I challenged myself to try haggis (a mix of sheep innards) while in Scotland, balut (fertilized duck or chicken embryo) in the Philippines, poutine (a pile of fries, gravy and cheese curds) in Quebec, Luwak coffee in Indonesia (coffee made from beans eaten and defecated by civets) and Vegemite (leftover brewer's yeast extract) when Down Under. I cannot say I loved any of these delicacies, but I enjoyed trying each of them for the adventure and bit of cultural immersion they provided. Unfortunately, I also enjoy trying the kinds of local artery-clogging offerings at state fairs, such as fried Oreos and fried Twinkies, though I am not promoting that here!

Post-50, I am less worried about my body's contours. We all know that it takes more effort to keep weight off as we age. So I wear larger sizes now. Oh well.

Sometimes I eat Ben & Jerry's ice cream or frozen yogurt for dinner. Or I try a new, outlandish recipe with ingredients I've never heard of before. Or I experiment with combining ingredients. Because I can. It is one outstanding benefit of having an empty nest.

My children were picky eaters. I probably enabled them. While they were still living at home, the cuisine I served my kids was relatively bland, like pasta with butter and cheese and veggies on the side or hidden in the sauce by employing a food processor. Or I would handle dinner like a short-order cook, accommodating each person's preferences. One of my children did not eat vegetables; the other did not eat fruit. I got both of them to eat raw broccoli by slathering peanut butter on it or hiding it in pesto or tomato sauce on spaghetti.

I am pleased to share that my daughter became a much more adventurous eater in adulthood. She travels extensively and tries the local cuisine wherever she goes. I certainly have not given up on my son's gustatory habits. I like to think I set a good example to my children, at least with respect to culinary exploration and adventure. I will admit that my taste for sweets did not serve them, or me, well.

I used to host elaborate, multi-course dinner parties, mostly to impress people and thereby make me feel better about myself. I was in a neighborhood cooking club for several years and still use some of the recipes from that time. When my children were young, my next-door neighbor and I would, once a week, alternate making a double batch of whatever we were preparing for dinner and share half with the other family. In this way, one time every other week I would not have to make dinner. It was a helpful practice we both enjoyed at a time when we were both ultra-busy with family obligations.

Food has another meaning for me in sobriety. An important acronym we are taught to abide by is HALT. To preserve our sobriety, we are warned to avoid being "Hungry, Angry, Lonely, or Tired," all of which can be triggers for recovering addicts and alcoholics. Therefore, I keep something to eat with me at all times. I am working on making that something always be an item that is nutritious and not just easy and full of empty calories.

Make a list of foods you would like to try, whether you would like to cook them yourself or find them at a restaurant. I keep a running list on my cell phone of restaurants I would like to try, and take an iPhone pic of recipes I come across that I want to use. When an opportunity to eat out comes up, I have ready ideas.

How does food bring joy to your life? Has preparing it become just a chore? Has eating it become just a means and not a pleasure? How can you change this dynamic? Go to a farmers' market and challenge yourself to make something out of an unfamiliar item. Or relish the taste of fresh summer corn and tomatoes, or whatever else is at its seasonal peak. Deliberately use all of your senses when enjoying food. Food can provide more than nourishment. It can foster connection with others, with the Earth, and with yourself.

As chef Paul Prudhomme says, "You don't need a silver fork to eat good food." The best, most nutritious food is unprocessed, and fresh fruits and vegetables generally cost less than packaged food. Make a commitment to yourself to allow food to be more than just mindless consumption. Let it be a source of health, pleasure, and fellowship with others.

· 6 ·

Learning and Teaching

*N*umerous studies show that mental challenges keep us sharp and may stave off Alzheimer's disease and related dementia. According to the National Institute on Aging:

> Staying cognitively active throughout life—via social engagement or intellectual stimulation—is associated with a lower risk of Alzheimer's disease. Several observational studies link continued cognitive health with social engagement through work, volunteering, or living with someone. Mentally stimulating activities such as reading books and magazines, going to lectures, and playing games are also linked to keeping the mind sharp.[1]

As one of my grandparents died of Alzheimer's disease, I imagine that I am at greater than average risk of succumbing to Alzheimer's later in life. Therefore, I strive to learn new things every day. I also play "Words with Friends," attend many lectures, and read a good deal. I am lucky to live in a metropolitan area where so many stimulating and free events take place. With the Internet, however, we all can widen our worlds, in ways big and small.

Why not start a book club? Or join one at your local bookstore or library? I have participated in online book clubs, though my beloved neighborhood book club will be celebrating 20 years together soon. Universities provide free lectures, and adult learning classes are more popular than ever. It is not hard to find ways to stretch your mental muscles or to learn new skills. I still have on my list of future endeavors my hope to learn how to propagate succulents successfully, but here are a few learning experiences I tried.

8. Exercising My Brain

The brain is a muscle, and I'm a kind of body-builder.

—Karl Lagerfeld

I was alarmed with the brain fog I experienced while pregnant. People assured me that my sharpness would return after the babies were born. Part of me wondered, as the years passed by, whether my mind would return to its pre-pregnancy performance level. I was especially doubtful when I looked at my children's high school math homework and it was incomprehensible to me. At those times, my brain appeared to be just mush.

When my children questioned why I did not remember something, I would respond, "The files are full." I think a lot of my absentmindedness came from constant multitasking and not doing things with careful intention. I used to be so proud of my ability to multitask. What I have come to realize, however, is that my multitasking prevented me from being fully present. I try very hard now to do one thing at a time, and the resulting focus has increased my productivity—counterintuitive to me, but true.

I vividly remember the time the pendulum swung from my thinking that my parents knew everything to thinking they knew nothing. I was fourteen years old at the time. I assumed my children had similar doubts about me during their teenage years.

To increase my work prospects, as well as to impress my children, I took the Maryland Bar exam. I was able to take a truncated version because I met certain provisions regarding years of practice as a member of a different state Bar. After the exam, another test-taker asked me which prep class I had taken. "I did not take one," I answered, as nausea of self-doubt rose in my throat.

But I passed! What a confidence booster that was for me. I refused to dwell on how I would feel if I had failed. And passing a bar exam as a middle-aged person gave me extra credibility with employers. It indicated that my brain was still working well, and gave me courage to keep attempting to conquer intellectual challenges. I was able to serve many more clients with this new credential.

Through scientific studies, we know that both nature and nurture affect brain function. We can stave off declining brain function by remaining physically active, maintaining a healthy lifestyle, reducing stress, and exercising our brains.

How might you challenge yourself intellectually? I have met middle-aged women who have returned to school to get their MBAs, JDs, or other professional degrees. I have met even more who have taken real estate exams to become realtors. Just as our bodies perform better with exercise, so too do our brains. Think about it.

9. Back to School

Education is not filling a pail but the lighting of a fire.

—William Butler Yeats

The adage that youth is wasted on the young—attributed to Irish dramatist George Bernard Shaw—really hits home with me when it comes to education. I love school. If I could do my college studies over now, I would be a much better student and would be so much more engaged in my classes.

One of the local universities offers continuing education classes. It seems that most colleges do so these days. And what a treasure it is for those of us who want to soak up new subjects. Often, classes can be taken on campuses or online.

I met bestselling author Iris Krasnow when she came to speak at my book club years ago. During that meeting, she told me about an idea for writing and other classes she would offer to women in transitional times of their lives. Years later, we fortuitously ran into each other, though I no longer believe there are any coincidences.

Iris was building a program at American University called LEAD, the Lifelong Education and Professional Development Program, designed to "provide adult learners with the impetus and writing/communication skills to help guide them through significant transitions in their personal and professional lives."[2] Her vision is that "participation in these courses help students make empowered choices as changes arise in family structures, with the growing independence of children, a return to the workplace and/or a desire to shift careers. Taught in an intimate setting, LEAD embraces students in a warm community with like-minded adult women who empower each other through personal and professional transitions."[3]

My favorite classes were her "Voices of Women" class and "Transformations: The Empowered Next Step." Some of my classmates took these classes multiple times.

The courses I took from Iris spurred me to write this book.

I felt a rush of excitement when I first stepped onto campus at American University for my first class. The classroom buzzed with the energy of middle-aged women who were hungry for learning. We bonded strongly during the course, and remain an enthusiastic support and resource group for one another. Iris generously hosts annual get-togethers at her riverside home for us to share ideas and camaraderie. And a Facebook group called the "Why Nots?" has been created by a few of my classmates to post periodic social outing opportunities that any one of us who is available can join.

I also took a digital media class at the university, led by her colleague, Kimberly Palmer. Kimberly helped me elevate my online presence and learn how to navigate new technology and platform applications.

My generation are "digital immigrants" when it comes to social media and other commonly used technology; today's young people are "digital natives," steeped in the techno world in which they grew up. Using technology is more intuitive for Millennials and Gen-Xers. They cannot conceive of a world that had no cell phones. My children and their friends were unfamiliar with the bulky machine called a typewriter that I took to school. They would laugh if they saw the mainframe computer we used in college. They are accustomed to carrying mini-computers, aka smartphones, in their pockets.

Even as an elementary school child, my cheeky son tried to charge me money for helping me with computer-related matters. At age ten, he was adept at fixing most of my issues with my computer and my cell phone.

We in the older generation do not need to be dinosaurs when it comes to modern technology. Resources abound, especially online. You just need to look for them. I am continually amazed with the how-to videos that populate YouTube. I had a problem with robins dirtying my car in my driveway with droppings every day, for example. A YouTube video instructed me to use towels to cover my side-view mirrors when parked. The robins moved on! Apparently, they like to preen in car mirrors. Who knew?

I also took writing classes at my local independent bookstore. It helps me hone my craft. And another set of eyes looking at anything one has written almost always can improve a piece of writing. In Malcolm Gladwell's book studying success, he posited that "ten thousand hours is the magic number of greatness."[4] I'm working toward that.

You may not have time to take a class right now. But you certainly have time to open your mind and learn something new online. I know people who have learned how to play musical instruments via lessons they found online. I learned online how to repair my refrigerator and to get birds to stop pooping on my car. Seriously. I solved both problems by what I learned on YouTube videos. Though I would recommend TedTalks for more advanced mental floss.

10. Radiohead

The crowning fortune of a man is to be born to some pursuit which finds him employment and happiness, whether it be to make baskets, or broad-swords, or canals, or statues, or songs.

—Ralph Waldo Emerson

For years, friends and family have told me that I should have a talk show. I have a habit of interviewing people, even strangers, and am adept at eliciting information. A woman I met at rehab tearfully told me I had an enormous capacity to make people feel welcomed, one of the nicest compliments I have received. A therapist had told me that I like to ask people questions to deflect them from asking me any, or to keep me from being introspective about the me I abhorred for so many years. Perhaps.

One day, a friend who hosted an FM radio show called *Inside Out* had me on as a guest. The radio show, on WPFW in Washington, D.C., was one that looked at politics, culture, and many other things through a lesbian, gay, bisexual and/or transgender ("LGBT") lens. When a show was done on parents of LGBT children, she extended me an invitation.

I jumped at the chance. It was fun. It was informative. It was a boost to my ego.

A short time later, she asked if I would like to be one of the hosts and producers. I accepted and have been doing my own shows once a month ever since.

I have interviewed the D.C. attorney general, members of the Gay Men's Chorus of Washington, parents of transgender youth, and many more. The shows are available on iTunes as a podcast,[5] as well as on the WPFWfm.org website.[6]

Live radio presents challenges. Sometimes a caller says something inappropriate or difficult to understand. There cannot be any on-air dead time, so I have to be ready with a comment or question at all times. Sometimes the studio equipment fails, or a guest is late to arrive. All of these happenings have helped me build skills and character.

Being on live radio has forced me to moderate the speed at which I talk, to breathe evenly, and to listen closely to others while they speak so that I ask good follow-up questions. I sounded unusually breathy during my first solo hosting gig, because I was so nervous.

My work on the show has increased my creativity and resourcefulness, and helped me understand and keep current on LGBT issues. I learned how to be more sensitive. I learned, for example, how to use gender-neutral pronouns and not to make assumptions about a person's preferred pronouns based on their appearance. My children tell me that, in some of their university classes, the professor begins each semester asking by what pronoun a student wishes to be addressed. Times are changing.

Although I already was an LGBT ally, my experience on *Inside Out* led me to join PFLAG[7] and to attend D.C. Pride, a festival and parade of support for the LGBT community.

Attendance at D.C. Pride also was mind-expanding. I had no idea how many gay organizations existed. I got leads and ideas for future radio show topics.

The joy on display at Pride was infectious. I carried a sign saying, "I love my gay AND straight children," which caused several groups of young gay people to hug me and thank me. Some relayed their stories of nonacceptance by their parents, which hurt my heart. I feel that I am doing my part to support the LGBT community and increase understanding.

I admit that part of my motivation for doing the LGBT radio show is to demonstrate to my gay son how much I support him and wish to be an advocate for the LGBT community. To date, he has not listened to my show. I cannot force him to do so. I must accept this thing I cannot change and remember I can only control my own actions and no one else's.

Learning about other people and what motivates them is one of my passions. This radio show provided me a vehicle to pursue a passion. I realize that I was lucky to have this opportunity come into my orbit, and that this particular activity may not be everyone's cup of tea. We can make certain opportunities for ourselves, however. The more doors we enter, the more doors open to us. We can do guest blogs, submit freelance articles, volunteer. What passion will you pursue next?

11. Consciousness Raising for Adults

Either write something worth reading or do something worth writing.

—Benjamin Franklin

My passion is writing. When things got rough in my life, I journaled. It was one way of working through my angst and worry. I also immersed myself in books as a means of escape. I was a voracious reader as a child, which certainly helped me then and in my professional life. Books provided me windows to wider worlds, fueled my imagination, and expanded my vocabulary. Like anything else, the more one writes, the better one becomes at it. Writing is an important part of my identity.

Journals are widely available today, and come in many sizes. Some people I know journal on their cell phones or computers. It is an effective vehicle for processing emotions, learning, and putting things in perspective. Journaling was mandatory when I was in rehab, and I would wager that most therapists and life coaches recommend keeping a journal. If I reread a journal of mine, it helps me see the progress I have made on a wide array of issues and goals, as well as the lessons I forgot but want to employ again.

Books help us stretch our minds and perspectives. I have wanted to contribute to society's dialogue on matters of importance to me, like combating racism, raising children, and self-actualization.

I dabbled in freelance writing when I was an at-home mom. I had put my legal career on hold because I wanted to do the best possible job raising my children. I also had a Norman Rockwellian notion that my childhood would have been different if my mother had not been in the working world.

The first time I was published was a big rush for me. It was in *Parenting* magazine. I had sent in a cathartic essay entitled, "How to Maintain Your Self-Esteem as a Stay-at-Home Mom." I did not follow the protocol, which typically involves sending a query letter to an editor first to see if the publication was interested in my idea, but got lucky that the right editor read my piece and liked it. This first article led to more assignments and submissions. At one point, I was on staff at a local magazine as a contributing writer and editor.

Then I set my sights higher. A lifelong dream of mine has been to get my own book published.

I got my first adult nonfiction book published, and learned how not to go about things in the publishing world. After my book, *Not the Cleaver Family: The New Normal in Modern American Families*,[8] was published, the publisher promptly went out of business. Just my luck. But because the book was such a labor of love about something for which I possess a great deal of interest, I enjoyed writing it. And I learned more about book publishing and marketing.

I interviewed hundreds of people for my book, and did most of my own marketing. I cared deeply about the subject of how the modern American family has changed in this decade and raising consciousness about microaggressions and indignities that continue today. People who belonged to the quickly emerging demographics I covered resonated with the issues explored and experiences chronicled in the book. Those who did not, but wanted to learn more about them, expressed elevated thinking as a result of my book. I was able to parlay the book into some fantastic speaking engagements.[9]

I wrote about mixed-race families, families led by same-sex couples, adoptive families, couples with singletons, single parents, and people who are child-free by choice. The subject of changes in the American family seemed to strike a chord, especially with those whose parents had been marginalized by society, as mine were, to a certain extent. My book talks have elicited dialogue that has both augmented my understanding and humbled me.

Initially, I was hesitant about being self-revelatory in my published writing. I rarely dealt willingly with issues of race for the first two decades of my life. I clearly do not appear to be white, though my father is Caucasian. Although my mother is Southeast Asian, most people assume I am Latina, and people speak to me in Spanish at least once a week. I did not want to draw attention to my differences and feeling of otherness and alienation. But gathering the stories of others whose families did not fit the cookie-cutter mold of a generation ago helped put my experiences in perspective. Exploring my racial identity was a luxury I had not previously afforded myself. As a result, I missed out on so much cultural richness. Once I dropped the self-consciousness of being biracial and shared with others of similar heritage, I experienced a catharsis of sorts. Completing my book was an affirming experience.

I learned to stop worrying about what others would think. This book is evidence of that. What would you do, if you were able to let go of being concerned with what other people thought of you?

What are some issues you care deeply about? You could start small by drafting an essay or short article about the object of your passion. Getting published today is much easier than when I started. There is an abundance of online opportunities and directories that tell you which publications accept which types of articles. Self-publishing books is simpler than it ever has been. My local independent bookstore has a self-publishing service. Amazon allows writers to publish e-books directly online.

If you decide to self-publish, you likely will have to do all of the marketing of your work. There are lots of online resources to help you navigate this necessary aspect of being an author today. Traditional publishers often help authors with marketing and sales, among other things, but they also expect authors to take a certain amount of initiative.

You can be heard by calling or writing to your public officials. Consider letters to editors or op-eds. Or communicate with your feet. Being part of a women's march was one of the most powerful experiences I have had in the last decade.

If you have something to say, say it! It is not too late. Laura Ingalls Wilder did not have her Little House books published until she was in her 60s. George Eliot's classic novel, *Middlemarch*, was published when she was 55 years old. Bram Stoker wrote *Dracula* when he was 50. Frank McCourt's *Angela's Ashes* came out when he was 66.

You, too, can be a literary late bloomer. As late bloomer William S. Burroughs said in his novel, *Junky*,[10] "When you stop growing, you start dying."

12. Consciousness Raising for Children

If a story is in you, it has got to come out.

—William Faulkner

Publishing my first children's book allowed me to return to looking at the world with a sense of childlike wonder again. Writing books that I wish had been available to me as a child was partially a healing exercise. The children's books I have written have dealt with issues close to my heart.

My first published children's book, *Mommy, Why's Your Skin So Brown?*, is a consciousness-raising book based on my experience of being frequently mistaken for the nanny of my lighter-skinned children. It grew out of an article I wrote for my local newspaper entitled, "Being a Parent Isn't Always Apparent,"[11] in which I implored readers not to let their curiosity overwhelm their manners. Several Washington, D.C., preschools distributed my article to their parent communities. I searched for a book to help me talk about the annoying and embarrassing situation my children and I often found ourselves in when strangers and even professionals assumed my children were not mine. I could not find one, so I wrote it myself. I did not want my children to internalize any feeling of something being wrong with our family, as I had felt as a child. This book, and open, continuing dialogue with my children, was part of my effort to prevent that sentiment from taking hold in my nuclear family.

It took me years to get it published. It actually was published during the year I turned 50. I had sent my draft to a few publishers, with no luck. A childhood friend then shared that she had gotten her children's book published with an indie publisher of children's books, Mirror Publishing, and suggested I give them a try, using her name as an introduction. The editor there liked my book and took it on. He said they accepted about 6 percent of the manuscripts submitted, so I felt fortunate to have made it through the door.

Mirror Publishing also accepted my second children's book, *Healing for Hallie*, about the importance of expressing one's feelings, something that took me decades to learn, at least when it came to things about which I felt guilt or shame. When I was a child in Catholic parochial school, there were some girls who were not allowed to come to my home because my parents were divorced and therefore excommunicated by the church at that time. I never told anyone then about the feelings this brought me. It would have been much healthier had I expressed how I felt, rather than carrying a yoke of shame for so many years. I suppose I wrote this book to my younger self.

I employed my friend's daughter to create the beautiful, evocative watercolor illustrations that accompany the text. Parents and social workers have told me that they have used this book with children to facilitate communication about emotions. When I read this book to schoolchildren, I am delighted to hear their comments.

I adore children and feel so blessed when I have opportunities to read my book to children in schools and bookstores. The message in my book about sensitivity to differences and the effect careless comments may have on others was so heartfelt, that reading the story aloud and putting it into the universe brought me joy.

Children are like sponges. They absorb so much around them. I would like to be part of the goodness children absorb. My first book may save someone from unintentionally inflicting harm via their words, or making false assumptions. My second children's book is used by parents, teachers, and therapists to help children process their feelings.

When I discuss my books with young people, more often than not, they will ask me questions about writing. So many of them like to create stories and want to know what it takes to be an author. Perhaps I will make a difference in a young person's life in this way.

Think about creative endeavors that bring you joy. Or that could do so, if you tried them. Sometimes we, especially as women raising children or in other caretaker roles, get so caught up in meeting the needs of others that we forget what we need. Make a list of things that elevate you. Start one of them. Today.

13. Empowering Women

> *What we think, we become.*
>
> —Buddha

Once I found my voice, I began cohosting women's empowerment and writing retreats. My retreat partner, Dr. Nicole Cutts, and I help women to develop as writers and speak their truth.

Each woman at our retreats wants to be a writer. By the time they leave, we make them say, "I am a writer." If we do not believe in ourselves, who will?

For the closing ceremony at our retreats, we had participants write on pieces of paper what holds them back from pursuing their writing dreams in earnest. Then we burned the papers, resolving to break through these obstacles. We set writing goals and signed up to be each other's accountability partners. We started a closed Facebook group to encourage each other and share ideas, tips, accomplishments, and frustrations. Several attendees have gone on to publish their dream books, and more are on the way.

There were tears from most of the participants with whom I met in private sessions during the retreat. So many of our sisters are walking wounded. There is a pervasive sentiment of not feeling good enough. Wake up! We are all perfectly imperfect and we all have scars and baggage. But the past need not define us. One cannot achieve what one will not try to do. I don't seek to survive this life; I seek to thrive.

Another way I seek to empower myself and other women is via political activism. During the last election, many of the women I knew felt fear that our commander in chief was known to have abused women, and the effect his election may have on our society. Gathering a group of women to join the Women's March on Washington helped us all feel less helpless. We continued to meet after the march to discuss other ways of making our voices heard.

Writing a letter to our congresspeople or calling their offices were ways we sought to make a difference. I participate in a weekly "Black Lives Matter" vigil in my predominantly white neighborhood when I can. Taking action is important, to effect change both in our society and within ourselves.

In our current political climate, taking action is perhaps even more important. I watched with horror when the white supremacists descended on Charlottesville, Virginia, a place for me of collegiality and learning. I attended law school there and it holds a special place in my heart. I shed tears learning of a young woman who was killed by a white supremacist angry at her opposition. I was stunned that citizens in a Jewish temple were surrounded by neo-Nazis in their place of worship. I cannot stand by and thereby be complicit in the hatred. German pastor Martin Niemöller's admonition continues to be true:

> First they came for the Socialists, and I did not speak out—
> Because I was not a Socialist.
> Then they came for the Trade Unionists, and I did not speak out—
> Because I was not a Trade Unionist.
> Then they came for the Jews, and I did not speak out—
> Because I was not a Jew.
> Then they came for me—and there was no one left to speak for me.[12]

There are many ways to combat hate and make a difference. We can take on racism and bigotry when we encounter it, one conversation at a time. We can confront hateful language when we hear it, in a respectful way. Buddhist teacher Jack Kornfield provides some ideas for how we can make a difference:

> For some your response may be reaching out to connect with those threatened, across lines of religion, race, class, sexual orientation. For some it may mean reaching out to the individuals and groups who are promoting hate and prejudice. For some it may mean educating others. For some it may mean political organizing, or activism, or standing up in peaceful ways in the midst of heated demonstrations.[13]

I hope to do my part in eradicating hate in our society, for my children's sake. The vitriol is reaching alarming levels.

We are not helpless and we have the ability to stand up and be heard. If not us, then who?

14. Sculpting a New Life

> *Every child is an artist. The problem is how to remain an artist once we grow up.*
>
> —Pablo Picasso

I find creating art to be meditative. For years, I had wanted to try sculpture. I finally found a class nearby that fit my schedule and my budget.

The instructor had us start by sculpting skulls. I had no idea that sculpting a human figure required awareness of bone and muscle structure. We received a mini course in anatomy during our first class. Sculpture takes much more knowledge and finesse than I had thought.

Later in the session, nude models were introduced to the class. It was startling at first, for me to see the models disrobe so nonchalantly and let a dozen people in a circle examine their bodies and try to replicate them in clay. The models' confidence, while stunning, was inspiring. It helped me shed another layer of self-consciousness.

The other students in the class were more adept than I was at sculpting realistic looking figures. At first I felt dismay. I learned not to compare my work negatively against that of others. Every real artist was an amateur first. We are where we are. A short version of the Serenity Prayer is "Oh, well."

I kept a couple of pieces I made during the course. They mostly elicit chuckles from visitors. The skull I made comes out at Halloween. It is slightly scary.

I had envisioned making grand sculptures for display in my home. I discovered I was not very good at it. I am glad I tried it, though. It increased my appreciation for fine sculpture—by others.

I also took the opportunity in my intentionally slower lifestyle to indulge my love of painting. I opened an Etsy online shop and even was able to sell a painting or two. At the least, I created things I considered beautiful and decorated my home with them. I am a little bit more adept at painting than sculpting.

Creating art allows us to view objects, people, landscapes, and just about everything in a different way. The number of styles and myriad of media available makes creating art an endeavor accessible to all. When traveling in third world countries, I have seen people make art out of garbage. I have seen planters made of used tires and plastic bottles. In an African art gallery, I bought an antelope head sculpture completely constructed out of aluminum soda cans.

While beautifying one's environment with art is a commendable endeavor, the process alone of creating art is healing. It is a sensory process. Remember how good it felt to finger paint when you were a youngster?

It does not matter if what you create is "good." We all know that beauty is in the eye of the beholder. It is the process of creating that can feed our spirits.

15. Stitchery

I'm always tinkering with something—suddenly I'll think I can work with wood, but then I'll realize I can't, so I go back to sewing.

—Melissa McCarthy

There is something in making things by hand that elevates my self-esteem. I bought an inexpensive used sewing machine on a Facebook online yard sale in my area and took up sewing.

I had not sewn anything since the 1970s, when my aunt enrolled me in a Singer sewing class at a local fabric store and I produced a few groovy outfits. I began this time around by sewing pillow covers that I filled with pillows I found at thrift shops or at Goodwill. I also sewed a loose-fitting, washable slipcover for a beat-up ottoman someone had given me. The fun fabric I found on Etsy provided a shot of color to the room I put it in and gave the ottoman new life.

Partially because of my semi-wild dog, whose puppylike energy seems to have little chance of dissipating any time soon, I have nothing precious or expensive around my house. And as much as can be is of the washable variety.

My stitches are not perfect, but they are serviceable, and I now can make things I do not wish to buy, and for a fraction of the cost. Plus, I have something to show for my labor that presumably will stick around for a while.

Do you have a craft or hobby you have wanted to try? Needlepoint was something easy for me to learn. I was not able to master knitting, however. . . .

16. Work It

> *Choose a job you love, and you will never have to work a day in your life.*
>
> —Confucius

With a certain amount of luck, perseverance, and resourcefulness, I found jobs I love. It suits me right now to have a flexible schedule so that I can write and travel to see my son's theater performances. Therefore, I currently have several part-time jobs.

I was able to marry my love of books and desire to learn new things with selling books at author events. I work part-time for the largest independent bookstore in Washington, D.C., and attend fascinating lectures for free at the events at which I work. I can choose which events interest me. This work has given me the chance to meet many of the authors, such as Malcolm Gladwell, Mark Shriver, Melanne Verveer, and former U.S. Supreme Court Justice John Paul Stevens. I have had opportunities to hear some of the greatest thinkers of our time such as, in my humble opinion, Hillary Clinton, Floyd Abrams, and Ta-Nehisi Coates. Hillary Clinton may be divisive on a political level, but she is the smartest person I have ever met. I was lucky to work with her on a legislative matter during her husband's first presidential term and was struck by her ability to absorb and command a tremendous amount of information. She has a brilliant intellect.

People's surprised reactions when they see me as a bookseller at author events say more about them than about me. Some of them know I got divorced and look at me with pity on their faces. Some treat me like the lowly hired help. The first time these things happened, they bothered me. They no longer do. I have internalized the lesson that what other people think about me is not my business.

I love books and am able to buy them at a deeply discounted price where I work. I get to know others who share my love of books and take classes by other authors. It is a buzzing literary and learning hub that has begun to host teach-ins on various issues. I am glad to be associated with this fine institution.

I also work part-time as an attorney for two law firms that don't just transfer money between corporate behemoths. They help real people with real problems. In one recent case, I represented an immigrant family–owned subcontractor against one of the biggest commercial contractors in Washington. While at the arbitration, the opposing counsel behaved in a smug manner, touting his client's overreaching contractual language. The arbitrator ruled in my client's favor. The amount of money my client received in the lawsuit represented a large percentage of the small company's annual revenue. It was a drop in the bucket for the commercial contractor. The clients were so very grateful and I was proud to represent them.

My other job is writing. Prior to this book, I published two children's books, one adult nonfiction book, and numerous articles.[14] When I do book talks, I sometimes receive a cash honorarium, and I usually have the opportunity to sell my books at the events. What I love most is the exchange of ideas I get to have with my readers. Freelance writing also provides extra income. Many publications and blogs pay freelancers, and I subscribe to free services that send me writing opportunities.[15]

One summer during college, I moonlighted as a house cleaner on Cape Cod. I also waitressed while a college student, and would do it again. As an older person these jobs would be physically harder to do than my current jobs. But I love food, talking to just about anyone, and seeing people get pleasure from food. Some people in the circles in which I used to socialize would likely look askance were I to become a food server. But honest work is honest work, and what other people think of me no longer governs my opinion of myself. I cannot change what others think, so I am challenged, as Viktor Frankl admonishes,[16] to change myself. The better I feel about myself, the less regard I have for external affirmation.

What are things you like to do? Many of my friends have started new jobs and careers after passing age 50. I know a woman who became a lawyer at age 70, and two who became nurses in their 40s. Several of my co-50-year-old friends started residential real estate and life coaching practices. I have a friend who left the law to start a music program for children, and another lawyer who left to start a cake shop. I have met executives who have left lucrative jobs to teach young students. We all have the ability to remake ourselves.

Do some research about what is available in your job market. Consider going on some informational interviews. I called a woman I know who had a cupcake food truck when I thought a mobile bakery might be something I would like to do. After meeting with her and learning about the permits required and the costs involved, I decided to pursue something else. But I would still be wondering about having a food truck if I had not at least made some inquiries.

TaskRabbit is a service that matches freelancers with local demand for help with everyday tasks and errands, including cleaning, moving, waiting in line, grocery shopping, deliveries, and handyman work.[17] More than 60,000 people work via TaskRabbit to provide consumers with immediate help from vetted, background-checked people. It is based on the idea of neighbors helping neighbors. "It's an old school concept upgraded for today," the company says. "We call it service networking, and it's changing everything."[18] Some who work with TaskRabbit parlay their freelance work into permanent positions; some use it between jobs and some simply like the flexibility of Task-Rabbit work when it fits their schedules.

If you like to do crafts or make things, Etsy makes it easy to sell your wares. I have sold a few paintings via Etsy.com. It is a nice way to support small businesses, too, if you need a gift for someone. The price points are generally lower than in retail marketplaces.

I generally do not enjoy selling things, but I dabbled in selling skin care products from home via Rodan and Fields. Some of my friends have success selling jewelry and accessories for Stella & Dot. I tried home sales, but did not love it. In the vein of life being too short, I gave away my inventory to someone who was better at sales.

Driving for Lyft or Uber is also a great way to supplement income with a flexible schedule. I met a widower who considered his Uber job a lifeline to the world. He was retired, with not much going on in his life at that point, and enjoyed meeting people via his driving job. I looked into being a driver for one of these services and another that was being launched for women only, but my car is not big enough (these services require four-door vehicles to be a driver and mine is only a two-door mini car).

Are you an amateur chef or good tour guide? Airbnb is now matching travelers up with people who provide cool experiences for travelers.[19] Service givers can be creative in their offerings, like offering prepared picnics, home-cooked meals, a session teaching anything you would like (for example, the history of a neighborhood or how to cook the specialty of the city you live in) or outings to whatever you like best about where you live. Talk about getting paid to do something you love!

If finances are not an issue, think about volunteering. There are many places that would benefit from your time and skills. Make a list of what interests you. For example, do you like working with children, with animals, with senior citizens? If you play an instrument or know how to do a craft, nursing homes often welcome visitors to share with their residents. One of my friends conducts collage-making sessions at a local assisted living facility. Another has read from her book at a nursing home. I really enjoy public radio, so I applied to volunteer at National Public Radio.

Maybe there is a nonprofit institution whose work aligns with your values. Most nonprofits can use help. TaskRabbit has a service called TaskRabbit for Good that connects their "taskers" with local nonprofits to work together to drive change and make a positive impact.[20]

Make a call or click online today. Make some extra money. Better yet, make a difference in the world, one day at a time.

17. Mixed Remixed

> *I am a story.*
>
> —MixedRemixed.org

"What are you?" Human? Definitely not what the questioner was seeking. Because I appear ethnically ambiguous, people sometimes let their curiosity overwhelm their manners.

It was not until after I turned 50 that I got to know lots of biracial people like me.

The Mixed Remixed Festival in Los Angeles is the largest gathering of mixed-race people in the United States. I learned about it from a friend who has biracial children. I applied to present my first book there, and was selected to be on a panel of mixed-race children's book authors. What I found was a home.

There were talking circles, workshops, films, poetry readings, topic panels, and music. The conversations were about shared experiences using language with nuances that differ for mixed-race people. We talked about how we navigate cultural identities. We discussed the double consciousness we employ outside of the festival. It was a place of deep learning for me, as well as where I finally felt understood.

I found my peeps at Mixed Remixed and plan to attend this affirming event every year. I learn more each time about navigating mixed heritage and racial terrain, and gain a stronger sense of belonging.

Where are your peeps? We all have a natural inclination to want to be with people like us, at least to a certain extent. Our melting pot country is rich with ethnic organizations and festivals, and even genetic communities.

Finding one's genealogy and genetics via such organizations as Ancestry.com and 23andMe has become popular for those who do not know much about their ethnic mix. Most people are much more racially mixed than they know. Have you spent time investigating your cultural roots and seeing how your people celebrate?

Former secretary of state Madeleine Albright learned at age 59 of her Jewish ancestry.[21] She was raised a Roman Catholic after her family fled Nazism. I suspect Jewish heritage was covered up by many who feared persecution during World War II.

Delving into the past can be a tricky thing. Maybe it should be called "Ancestry.Do-You-Really-Want-To-Know" instead of Ancestry.com. My friend who works for an adoption organization has seen DNA testing complicate many lives, for example, when affairs or other family secrets are revealed.

Are you interested in exploring your cultural heritage? Attendees at the Mixed Remixed festival who had tested their DNA for clues about their genetic backgrounds told me about finding birth parents or learning that who they thought were their parents were not. Some learned about Native American ancestry of which they were previously unaware. One learned that her grandfather, who had given her father up for adoption many years ago, lived right down the street from her.

It may not be necessary or desirable to do a DNA test, but there are many other ways to learn about your ancestry and the ways of the people from whom you came. I wish that I had taken some oral histories from my grandparents and other relatives when I had the chance. The Smithsonian Institution in Washington, D.C., is a repository of a great deal of cultural information and artifacts. There are cultural centers for many ethnicities in most urban areas and much information online. Have you ever explored the stories of your grandparents or other kin? What will you learn?

Social Activities

$\mathscr{H}$uman beings are social beings. Isolation is anathema to an alcoholic, and to people in general. Research shows that remaining socially engaged can maintain brain vitality and possibly stave off dementia.[1] According to the Alzheimer's Association, "research found that sports, cultural activities, emotional support and close personal relationships together appear to have a protective effect against dementia."[2] Because one of my grandmothers had early onset of Alzheimer's disease, I personally strive to stay active physically, mentally, and socially, to reduce my chances of a similar fate.

18. Dating for Dowagers

> *Don't look for a partner who is eye candy. Look for a partner who is soul food.*

—Karen Salmansohn

What does dating look like for those of us over 50? What is our ideal in a partner? While before it may have been "bad boys," head-turners, or those who could offer us financial security, for most women I know, kindness tops the list in this chapter in our lives. But how would I find appropriate gentlemen with whom I would like to keep company?

I had a brief foray into online dating sites, with little luck. Before getting advice from more seasoned chums, I would accept dates based on the assumed veracity of the candidate's profile. I wanted to believe the embellished profiles, reading them as if they were a high-end catalog or a well-written menu. One guy's photo was at least 10 years younger than he appeared when we met. In the photo, he had hair. In person, he was bald. I do not mind baldness. I do mind the dishonesty in his presentation, however. This guy also overshared intimate details about his life on the one and only date we had, and invited me to go away on a trip with him on his private plane to Machu Picchu. Then he told me he was still married but his wife had denied him sex for years. I was, for once, happy to be short because I was able to dodge his attempt at kissing me good night at the end of our date.

My second Match.com date was pleasant, until the man started expounding on how women should behave, in his opinion. As a fairly unedited person, I am a fan of strong opinions, but I felt as if I had stepped into a time warp while listening to his conservative views. I knew he was not someone with whom I would like a second date.

Disenchanted by my online dating experiences, I changed strategy. A girlfriend suggested I try speed dating. There is an organization in many metropolitan areas called Professionals in the City. They organize events and group them by age range and other categories. I first attended a reception for people over 50. It was disappointing, so I planned to try a speed dating event with my friend. One boring evening, however, I saw online that one was being held nearby, so I jumped in my car and decided to give it a try.

The room crackled with excited conversation, as people tried to make memorable first impressions. Four minutes were allotted to the singles, who ranged in age from young 20s to early 50s. The name Professionals in the City implied that attendees were "professionals" of some sort, though that was not always the case.

It was a fascinating microcosm of social interaction. It was ethnically and racially diverse. Guests were invited to stay after the speed dating portion of the evening to mingle and dance. Hookups did take place, and couples were able to connect online via the organization's website, if they wished—or not.

Though some of the speed dating events are separated by age range or other categories, the first one I happened to go to was not. The women are seated at small tables. Every four minutes, a bell rings, signifying that it is time for the men to rotate to a new table. The first man to sit at my table was young enough to be my son. He said he thought I was in my 20s. I showed him my license and he seemed shocked. Made my night.

I was flattered by the few men I met who were young enough to be my son yet earnestly tried to interest me in a date. They were not deterred when I showed them my license with my birth date. I ended up coaching two of the youngsters on how to beef up their opening lines and job descriptions when meeting prospective women.

I found the whole thing fascinating. I enjoyed seeing how a man would present himself in four minutes. Afterward, guests were invited to hang around for drinks and dancing. The mating ritual on display. I planned to write an article about the evening, but my editor wanted a first-person account. I was unwilling at that time to be that self-revelatory.

I met only one man that night who held my interest with his easy conversation and interesting profession. We ended up dating for almost a year after that night, though it ended badly.

I went as a "wing woman" with a girlfriend to some other speed dating evenings. She did get a good date or two with a charismatic Irish doctor out of the event.

After my breakup with speed date number one, I went to a speed dating event for people with advanced degrees. I figured I would at least meet intelligent men that way, and longed for some intellectual conversation.

No one exactly wowed me during their five-minute allotted interview/ audition time. But afterward, a pleasant enough Parisian who had been in the musical table rotation asked me to have a drink with him after the event. I told him I did not drink alcohol and he said he did not drink much. He regaled me with stories of the jobs he had held all over the world, including being a scuba diving instructor, a member of the French army, and a deliverer of six-figure luxury goods to their owners. He was a PhD candidate and his dissertation, which dealt with bicultural individuals, fascinated me.

We dated for several months. It lasted into the summer. My college-aged daughter was visiting one weekend and agreed to come with us for dinner on the boat of a French couple. It was a wonderful dinner, but my daughter was not impressed with my date. As we drove away she remarked, "That was the most arrogant man I have ever met."

"But we have such wonderful, wide-ranging, intellectual, mind-expanding discussions," I replied.

"Mom, you can get that from your girlfriends. You don't have to date it."

After that evening, I started to notice the arrogance. The relationship began to unravel. It ended shortly thereafter.

I still recommend speed dating to friends who are newly on the dating scene. I believe it is easier to get a true feeling about someone when meeting face-to-face, as opposed to online. If I ever returned to the dating scene, however, I would have iChats or Skype meetings with anyone before agreeing to meet them for a date. I think body language and facial expressions can reveal important things about one's character.

Putting myself out there in the dating world felt vulnerable and risky. Since people over the age of 50 do not usually hang out in bars (or if they did, I would be unlikely to want to meet them), online dating or other methods that might cut through 10 dates' worth of info on a person is an efficient way to go. Women are somewhat at an advantage in the online dating scenario, in that the sites typically allow women to use them free of charge, or at least at a lower cost than for men.

I know people who met via an online dating site and are happily married. I have met more happily married couples who met their partners while simply going about their business. According to a local running club in the D.C. area, 50 couples met while participating in the club's running events and ultimately married. Shared interests may be the best way to meet, for obvious reasons.

Although I did not find a true love while online or speed dating, I figured out what I wanted and did not want in a relationship. I learned that I was ready to date again, even as someone in middle age.

I now know that I had to develop a healthy self-esteem before I could be in a healthy relationship. I also had to learn the difference between being in love with an image of what I wanted and being in love with who was really there.

Now that I am in a solid, loving relationship, I have adopted another affirming practice: every day, my partner and I text to each other one thing we appreciate about the other person. Sometimes it is about something small, like his smile. Other times it is about feeling heard and supported. It doesn't really matter what exactly it is. The practice helps me keep looking for the things I like about him, instead of focusing on what I do not like. If I look for the negative and spend my mental energy there, it will become magnified. I would much rather magnify the good in my significant other. I am sure you would, as well. This technique also helps when one's teenagers are going through trying stages. . . .

If you have a partner, what do you appreciate about him or her? Make a list and share it. Who doesn't like feeling appreciated? Keep the list and look at it when a rough patch comes along. If you do not have a partner, what are the qualities you most value in another?

19. Beat that Drum

> *Each woman . . . arrives there through deep meditation, dance, writing, painting, prayermaking, singing, drumming, active imagination, or any activity which requires an intense altered consciousness. . . . She arrives there by deeply creative acts, through intentional solitude, and by practice of any of the arts.*
>
> —Clarissa Pinkola Estes[3]

Before I turned 50, I was not familiar with drum circles. I first participated in one at a rehab facility. I was self-conscious trying it, at first, and then allowed myself to melt into the flow and rhythm. The experience seemed to have some healing properties, which makes sense to me since we each emerged into this world first hearing the beating of our mother's hearts in utero. The drum circle definitely helped solidify our community of participants.

Drum circles usually are informal, with no leader. The main objective is to get in tune with each other and one's self. A group consciousness may be formed via the circle.

A drum circle in D.C.'s Meridian Hill Park has taken place every Sunday for more than 50 years. It is believed to have started during the week of Malcolm X's assassination in 1965, as a spiritual revival.[4] It was at that time about black cultural awareness, when the surrounding neighborhood was predominantly African American.

The first time I ventured into Meridian Hill Park, I was struck by the many hues of skin color of those present at the drum circle. People were there from varied walks of life, joining on a Sunday afternoon in the park to dance or beat on just about any surface. I could feel the drumbeat in my chest and under my feet. The group sound seemed to take on physical presence. If anyone remained still, I wager that it took some effort.

Drum circles used to be popular only among counterculture groups. The practice has spread beyond, in this decade.

I came upon a drum circle on Venice Beach one day. It seemed to have started impromptu. A large crowd gathered. The energy was contagious. My friend and I found ourselves drawn in to the rhythm and the dancing. It was a fabulous way to spend a few hours unwinding on the beach. No talking was necessary. We all just let ourselves get carried away with the beat. I did not know anyone but my one friend there. I let go.

Do you allow yourself to let go? Have you tried the cathartic feeling of drumming? You don't even need a real drum to try it. A pot or pan would work. Overturned plastic paint buckets make excellent substitute drums. In rehab, one counselor had me beat large pillows with a baseball bat to get my frustration and anger out. It worked.

20. Sing Like No One's Listening

I don't sing because I'm happy; I'm happy because I sing.

—William James

When my children were little, they would cover their ears when I sang. Harrumph.

So maybe I do not have the best voice. So what? I challenged myself to sing in front of others at an open mic event. This was in the vein of "dance like no one's watching." I did it more to overcome my embarrassment than to show my "talent."

I had done karaoke with a group on stage before. This was different. I was alone in the spotlight. People were looking just at me.

I did it. I cannot say I enjoyed it, but I had the guts to try it. Moving beyond my comfort zone helps me grow and makes the next new thing—whatever that may be—easier to try. And one can find karaoke venues just about anywhere. While you are unlikely to see me on stage any time soon, I am an enthusiastic supporter and listener.

21. Third Eye

> *A Senegalese poet said, "In the end we will conserve only what we love. We love only what we understand, and we will understand only what we are taught." We must learn about other cultures in order to understand, in order to love, and in order to preserve our common world heritage.*
>
> —Yo-Yo Ma

I bought a sari when I was in Nepal. I attended my first traditional Indian/Nepali Hindu marriage ceremony and was happy to wear it. I felt that my wearing of the sari, and the bindi, were signs of respect in this context.

I wondered, however, whether this was a form of cultural appropriation or misappropriation? Cultural misappropriation is a debate that has begun to dominate the media. It is the adoption of cultural elements in a colonial manner—elements are copied from a minority culture by members of a dominant culture, and used outside of their original cultural context. It is particularly disrespectful when the person copying something from another culture makes no attempt to learn about the meaning of the thing in question.

Author and Fordham law professor Susan Scafidi defines cultural appropriation as taking, without permission, intellectual property, traditional knowledge, cultural expressions, or artifacts from someone else's culture. "This can include unauthorized use of another culture's dance, dress, music, language, folklore, cuisine, traditional medicine, religious symbols, etc. . . . It's most likely to be harmful when the source community is a minority group that has been oppressed or exploited in other ways or when the object of appropriation is particularly sensitive, e.g. sacred objects."[5]

As a person of color, I am especially mindful of cultural sensitivity. Our multicultural society makes it somewhat inevitable that many things will be shared among groups present in this country. Of course, it should be done with respect.

Thus, I spent time learning about saris and investigating the meaning of the bindi. Saris are worn by women throughout India, Nepal, Bangladesh, and Sri Lanka. They are one of the oldest types of garments still in use. A sari is made of several yards of fabric draped over the body. It takes a while to learn how to wrap a sari properly, and different methods and styles are used in various South Asian regions.

A bindi is a popular forehead decoration worn mainly in South Asia, from an old Hindu tradition. The word bindi is derived from a Sanskrit word and is associated with a person's mystical third eye. Bindis have been used to ward off bad luck, to remind Hindus to cultivate their spiritual vision, and to signify that a woman is married. They have transformed over time to become popular fashion accessories.

There is, I know, a fine line between appreciation and appropriation, and I do not wish to cross it. My hosts at the Hindu wedding service said that they appreciated my adopting their traditional garb for the occasion. It felt right to me, in any event. It felt graceful and elegant. I wore this fashion that was unusual to me as a sign of respect. But this activity helped me gain respect and understanding as well.

Expand your horizons. Learn about other cultures. Keep growing.

22. Ordinary People

The energy you'll expend focusing on someone else's life is better spent working on your own. Just be your own idol.

—Sophia Amoruso

John F. Kennedy Jr. was two feet from me, seated behind me at a wedding I attended in New York City in the early 1990s. He looked like an Adonis. During the ceremony, I turned around and he was right behind me. I froze. During the reception, we crossed paths several times, yet I could not even speak. We reached for hors d'oeuvres from the same tray at one point and I babbled something unintelligible. Why? Because he was stunningly attractive and I had put him on a pedestal of somehow being better than I was.

Flash forward two decades. I was sitting in a coffee shop in Venice Beach, California. Actor Tobey Maguire walked in and sat down at the table next to mine. I had loved him in the Spider-Man movies, and *The Great Gatsby* was soon to premiere with him in a lead role. Because of the work I had done on myself, there was no star-struck response in me. He was more handsome in person than he was to me on screen. He had come to the coffee shop to interview potential nannies and personal assistants. I eavesdropped on his first interview with a young nanny candidate.

After she left, I turned to him and said, "You are asking the wrong questions." He then started asking me for ideas. Some of mine included asking what the candidate would do in a hypothetical emergency scenario, what kinds of activities she would do with the children, her driving record status, her thoughts on how much television kids should be permitted to watch under her care, among others. He liked what I had to say, and asked if I would give him my contact information to potentially interview for the personal assistant position. I declined, saying that I was far too overqualified! At that point, he may have thought I was a crazy person. But it was a fun conversation between two people who appeared to hold each other with equal regard.

One thing I took away from Gabrielle Bernstein's *Spirit Junkie*[6] was the important lesson of not elevating other people's status above your own. When we put people on pedestals and idolize them, fear and ego tinge our encounters with them. We set ourselves up to feel less than, even though we know, intellectually, that we are all equal human beings.

We live in a celebrity culture that can skew our values. The whole "VIP" notion that our society espouses in certain arenas can warp our perspectives.

Because I am now comfortable in my own skin, I do not tend to elevate other people anymore. This change in dynamics in my daily interactions has improved the quality of all of my encounters which, today, includes corporate legal clients who may think they are of a more important stature than I.

As a recovering codependent, I also have to practice nonattachment in my personal relationships. I work hard at not subjugating my needs and keep communication clear to do so. We each have our own Higher Powers, and each are responsible for our own happiness and well-being, as are other people.

Do you sometimes elevate your estimation or treatment of people for the wrong reasons? Is there any other aspect of your treatment of others that you would like to change? Awareness is the first step toward changing anything. You can do it.

23. Nothing Like Old Friends

I've learned that people will forget what you said, people will forget what you did, but people will never forget how you made them feel.

—Maya Angelou

As a Girl Scout, we sang the verse *"Make new friends, but keep the old; one is silver and the other gold"* over and over. I was too young to appreciate its significance at that time. I do now.

At one point in my life, I was more about breadth than depth. I spread myself too thinly. My best friends remain those who have known me the longest. The shared history binds us together in profound ways.

My besties from high school have loved me through thick and thin, and I them. The day I got divorced, they spent the night at my house. I have no biological sisters. These friends are my chosen sisters. We go away on mini-vacations together, periodically. We laugh together until our stomachs hurt.

My ex-sister-in-law is my best friend. Decades ago, we both married brothers from a family with difficult-to-navigate parameters and lots of unresolved issues. We are uniquely positioned to understand certain dynamics at play in our lives as part of this family. I thank God that she is in my life.

Our sad reality today is that she has metastasized cancer. She was five years clear of breast cancer before it returned with a vengeance. Every day I have with her is a gift. I feel that every day. She has come to visit me between chemo treatments, and hosts me at her home frequently. She recently gave me the nicest compliment I have ever received. She said, "You sometimes refer to our relationship as being like sisters, but you are better than that; you are my best friend. We don't have the baggage that comes with sisters."

I also have sisters in sobriety. My sponsor and women I have come to know in the 12-step rooms have saved my life. They loved me until I could love myself. Part of recovery is helping other alcoholics. We are always there for each other, even in the middle of the night. I can call my sponsor—and my sponsees can call me—at any hour for guidance or support. When I cannot reach my sponsor, I call other women in the program. I can tell them my darkest secrets and never feel judged or crazy, but rather lightened and understood. These women are my chosen family.

I will spend this chapter of my life nurturing the relationships most important to me. There are many levels of friendship, and I intend to enjoy whatever time I have left with these chosen sisters. No longer will I spend my time indiscriminately, but rather intentionally, with those who deserve and respect me. Avoid time vampires. Time is the one thing we cannot get back. Guard it wisely.

· 8 ·

Physical Challenges and Well-Being

$\mathcal{W}$e know that physical activity is beneficial to our health. We also know that most of us cannot easily perform at the same level in our fifth decade as we could in our second or third. But physical decline is not inevitable once we turn 50.

I definitely have gained weight as I have aged, and it is much harder to lose weight when I want to shed a pound or two. I used to be so active—and blessed with speedier metabolism—that I could pretty much eat whatever I wanted and not gain weight. That is no longer the case.

Menopause also can slow us down. The average age for menopause is between 45 and 55, and the effects of menopause can be daunting. Increased body fat, memory problems, hot flashes, decreased libido, depression, and high blood pressure are some of the symptoms we experience as the hormonal changes occur. While my body fat percentage definitely has risen, I am relieved to no longer have to deal with having a period.

Pat Wingert, journalist and coauthor of *The Menopause Book*,[1] describes menopause as a time of personal empowerment:

> For most women, reaching menopause is a major wake-up call. Reaching this milestone makes it hard to ignore the fact that you're getting older. But that doesn't mean you surrender to it. I think the best way to respond is to embrace the idea of being a more active participant in your own health. We all know what we should do: get more exercise, eat better, drink less and sleep more—but many of us put off these things until "tomorrow." Well, menopause is a reminder that "tomorrow" is here. If you want to age as well as possible, you need to make these changes now. After all, studies show that your health at midlife is a good predictor of how well you will age.

Smart women make a point of educating themselves about all the changes that their bodies are undergoing at this phase of their lives, so they can respond in the best ways possible. After all, if you know what to expect, and why it's happening, you can make well considered decisions about your health and how you want to age.

The tricky part is figuring out reliable sources for this information. The internet is full of sites that want to sell you things you don't need or that are actually harmful. Look for reliable sources of information and remember that if something sounds too good to be true, it probably is. You need to be your own best advocate.

It may surprise you to learn that studies show that many women consider their 50s to be the best or happiest decade of their lives. We know who we are, we know what we want, and we're not afraid to go after it. We often have more control over our lives and are more sure of ourselves. But an important lesson of midlife is to make sure you carve out more time for you and make changes that will help ensure that you continue to be healthy and active so you can continue to be the person you want to be. That means learning more about what's happening to your body. Getting more exercise to maintain cardiovascular health, flexibility, balance, and strength. Making sure you get physicals and health screenings so any problems that pop up are dealt with early and promptly. In short, be as mindful about your own health as you are about the health of those you love. Remember that taking good care of yourself increases the chances that you'll continue to be there for all the people you love.[2]

I am heeding Wingert's admonitions as I enter this phase of my life, and having fun while doing it.

24. Silent Disco Party

There is something so rewarding about dancing. It's almost spiritual—you let loose, you feel free, you get endorphins from the exercise.

—Julianne Hough

We donned our earphones to tune into the same playlist. Then we danced with reckless abandon in the middle of a park/traffic circle in Washington, D.C.

A group in D.C. that I met via their free yoga offerings has a unique mission in our nation's capital: "WithLoveDC is a movement to spread love, joy, and acceptance throughout the District. Join us in our mission to make this world a better place, one smile, hug, or random act of kindness at a time."[3] It was started by a remarkable young woman, Heather Markowitz, whose presence in my life is such a gift. She epitomizes for me the kind of life I would have liked for myself in my 20s, and the joy I am infusing my life with now.

One of the fun activities they periodically organize is a silent disco party in Dupont Circle, an urban park in the middle of a busy traffic circle. I know how important it is to remain active as I age, but I seek new forms of exercise now, and do not enjoy spending a lot of time in a gym. Dancing is a much more fun way for me to work up a sweat.

Participants in the silent disco parties go to the group's website and download a playlist of music. At the appointed start time, we put on our own headphones or earbuds, start our music, and start dancing. Hilarity ensues. We are all crazily boogieing around the circle and only we can hear the music. Talk about dancing like no one is watching. . . .

WithLoveDC also organizes "adult recess" sessions around town. Participants meet at the appointed place and time and play tag, hide and seek, leapfrog, or whatever. The point is unadulterated fun.

If you do not know of any groups in your area that do fun things, check out Meetup.com. Meetup brings people together in thousands of cities "to do more of what they want to do in life."

> It is organized around one simple idea: When we get together and do the things that matter to us, we're at our best. And that's what Meetup does. It brings people together to do, explore, teach and learn the things that help them come alive.
>
> For example, people run marathons, thanks to running Meetups. They write, thanks to writing Meetups. They change their careers, thanks to career Meetups. Because at Meetups, people welcome each other. They talk, help, mentor, and support each other—all in pursuit of moving their lives forward.[4]

I attended a lecture at National Geographic in which the researcher, who studied happiness, found that those who join groups are generally happier.[5] Moreover, by joining something, you may allow yourself the opportunity to enjoy pure, childlike fun.

What is the point of life if you do not allow yourself to have fun? If you worry that you have too much to do to take time for silliness, you may not realize that productivity often increases when we allow ourselves leisure and recreational time.[6] Besides, if we keep postponing doing something fun until the right time, it may never come.

Maybe there is a group activity you would like to try out. The Internet makes it so much easier to search for what is available, wherever you live. Take a look. It may just change your life.

25. Yogi

Yoga allows you to find an inner peace that is not ruffled and riled by the endless stresses and struggles of life.

—B. K. S. Iyengar[7]

I incorporated a yoga practice into my life. I especially enjoy doing yoga outdoors. Free yoga is offered outside via With Love DC[8] at the U.S. Botanic Garden, and in the majestic Kennedy Center by another group. When I was in Manhattan, I took advantage of the free yoga offered in New York's Bryant Park, and attended by hundreds. Yoga has gone mainstream.

There are many levels and styles of yoga offered in studios that have cropped up all over our country, as well as online. I have tried aerial yoga, "primal" yoga, hot yoga, dance yoga, and acroyoga, as well as the more traditional types such as Ashtanga and Vinyasa. I signed up this fall for a yoga triathlon with an organization called Wanderlust, which involves running five kilometers and then doing yoga and meditation.[9] I have seen yoga classes involving poses on standup paddleboards in water, but have not tried them—yet.

One need not be in good shape or athletic to start a yoga practice. Most teachers encourage yoga students to go at their own paces, to modify poses and rest as necessary. As one of my yoga instructors says, the best thing about yoga is that it is supposed to feel good.

Yoga is now accessible to all. My local studio has "gentle yoga," "super gentle yoga," and restorative yoga classes, as well as very advanced classes or specialized classes, such as yoga for those who suffer from depression. Prenatal yoga has become more popular, as has yoga for children. Some yoga classes are akin to simple stretching instruction. Once you learn a few poses, you can practice at home for as long or as little as you like. Or you can learn yoga online, via books, or on television, though I feel buoyed by the vibration of doing yoga with others.

The physical and mental benefits of yoga have been widely publicized, and most cities and towns are populated with yoga studios. Yoga practice is credited with easing stress and hypertension, and a panoply of other ailments. Its meditative aspects benefit the mind as well.[10] And it is good for your body, yielding increased flexibility and better digestion, for example. One of my friends claims that she is an inch taller since incorporating yoga into her life (probably by improving her posture). Simply doing the warrior pose makes me feel fierce and more ready to face whatever I need to do.

Yoga is not supposed to be competitive, though I have felt that vibe in a couple of studios and tried to ignore it, or moved to another studio. Find a place where you are comfortable.

The first time I joined in the group chant of "om," I felt a little self-conscious. The sacred Sanskrit mantra om is frequently uttered together at the beginning or end of a yoga class. It is a word difficult to define, but it encompasses the interconnectedness of all. It is a resonant sound that I can feel deeply in my chest. The hum of the extended sound vibrates between the lips. It feels cleansing and unifying when I give it my all. And uniting with other voices in this way can be a powerful experience.

The lovely word "namaste" is usually said together at the end of yoga classes. It is a sign of respect and gratitude. Translations differ, but it loosely means, "the light in me honors the light in you"—a lovely sentiment that always makes me smile.

One of my yoga teacher friends, Rebecca Elsen, calls doing good works yoga in action. I like to think about that when I am helping another person or doing another kind of good deed.

Yoga master Swami Satchidananda calls one of yoga's main teachings to "free yourself from depending on people, possessions, and even events for your happiness, and to realize and experience the true happiness that comes from within."[11] I definitely feel more energized after doing yoga and grateful that I was able to practice this act of self-care. I consider yoga a time-out from everything (cell phones are verboten) and gift to myself.

Jeff Krasno cofounded Wanderlust, a series of large-scale festivals around the world that combine yoga and wellness with the arts.[12] He calls Wanderlust's approach to yoga an "overarching principle for living" that incorporates a lifestyle of "practice, consuming ethically, eating locally, and living an inspired life."[13] Many in the yoga field use the word "mindfulness" when it comes to yoga. In these ways, the yoga lifestyle will be something I intend to keep in my life for the rest of my days.

I splurged on a yoga retreat, to lovely Costa Rica. My ex-sister-in-law, who was between cancer treatments, wanted to go, which helped me self-justify the cost, and Costa Rica was on my bucket list. I did some research and found a retreat on the less expensive side.

Costa Ricans speak of their culture as "Pura Vida." Simply translated, it means "Pure Life." To Costa Ricans, however, it has a much deeper meaning. It is a way of living a peaceful, simple life and an expression of eternal optimism, whatever one's circumstances may be. And it is contagious. I challenge everyone to try to spend some time in Costa Rica to try to absorb this omnipresent outlook. Pura Vida encapsulates the life philosophy I want to tend.

A taxi driver related to me a widely held belief among his countrymen: When Hitler was looking at a map, a fly was covering Costa Rica, which spared them from Hitler's wrath. Costa Rica emerged unscathed from World War II. Similarly, the big earthquake of 1987 had the same intensity it had in surrounding countries, but spared their country any significant damage. The Costa Ricans believe that their positive energy breeds good fortune. They claim to have no sharks, and the country has no army. They don't need one. Somehow, their neighboring countries' drug trade bypasses Costa Rica.

An interesting thing happened during the retreat to a participant who had many complaints (about a lack of hot water in her shower, the class not being of a style she liked, etc.). During one of the yoga classes, she pushed herself far too hard and was injured. She was taken away by an ambulance, and her trip was cut short. Was this a coincidence? Or a result of karma?

The delightful yoga instructor on the retreat, Rebecca Bly, gave me some new language I incorporated into my daily discourse. "Add a little sugar to the movement," she would say during yoga. I like the notion of adding sweetness to what we do each day, figuratively speaking. We do not know how much time we have left in this life. Why not make our time as sweet as it can be?

"If it is interesting to you, join me in this variation," was another of Rebecca's favorite phrases. With this, she reminded me of the need to accept people where they were. We all have different gifts and abilities. Who says one way is the right way? I need this as a frequent reminder.

While in Costa Rica, we also zip-lined above the trees. It was thrilling! We saw monkeys as we flew by. I even flew upside down! One of the playful zip-lining guides sort of tricked me into doing that, but it was exhilarating.

My typically adventurous sister-in-law was very fearful as we climbed the platform to begin zip-lining. I was surprised. We talked about it afterward. Because she has had to face her mortality due to metastasized cancer, she is less willing to compromise her safety. She has three adult children and would like as much time on this earth as possible. She pushed herself to complete the zip-lining course, however, and I was so proud of her.

Even though I am fearful of heights, I was not scared during the zip-lining. I am no longer afraid of death, not in a throw-caution-to-the-wind sort of way, but in an uninhibited, open-to-adventure sort of way. Now that my children are adults, I believe they can thrive without me if something were to happen. The lessons I want to impart to them are in my writings, if they wish to read them, and in my living amends to them. I am drinking fully from the cup of life now. I'm free and willing to live la Pura Vida!

Yoga is such a positive, affirming experience for me. It is meant to bring flexibility, balance, and strength to one's body and centeredness to one's mind. It reminds me to slow down and to guard against negativity.

Yoga can be a way of life. My friend Pleasance Silicki has used yoga to form "a community of people who thrive to live well and nourish all the relationships in their lives."[14] Her life mission is "to inspire communities and create meaningful connections through yoga, play, meditation, journaling, reflection, laughter, and honest conversations."[15] She started her organization, "lil omm," out of "a deep desire to connect with like-minded women who felt as passionate about yoga as they did their families," and encourages others to find communities *or* to create them if they cannot find them.[16]

> Sometimes it can be hard for people to be vulnerable, to reach out for help. But I know that every time I reach out and say, "Hey—I need some help over here with this life stuff!" other women nod in agreement and inspire me. I have a lot of faith and trust in the ancient wisdom—Ayurveda, yoga, meditation, Buddhist philosophy—and I have seen profound shifts in my own life as a result of my studies and application. Finding our way home to our true nature, simplifying our lives and connecting with others—these are essential to well-being in our modern world. And yoga is one way to explore these topics.[17]

Pleasance has many devotees in the Washington, D.C., area, where she teaches stress reduction and healthy habits via a course she calls "Thrive" that explores intentional living, yoga for women classes, sacred circles, and retreats. I am signed up for her "Pause" yoga and meditation retreat this fall.

Pleasance is an amazing teacher who radiates joy and groundedness. I am grateful our paths have crossed.

I find that most people who practice yoga are more present and centered. They are drawn toward gentleness of spirit. It is a community that I want in my life, especially now. I hope you will join a community of yogis near you.

26. Who Rescued Whom?

> *People always joke that "dog" spells "god" backwards. They should consider that it might be the higher power coming down to see just how well they do, what kind of people they are. The animals are right here, right in front of us. And how we treat these companions is a test.*
>
> —Linda Blair

More often than not these days, I wake up with a hairy male panting on my face, and sometimes licking it. Then he uses his paws to pull the covers off of me. Though I generally do not enjoy being woken up, I cannot resist my Lab mix's exuberance for life—and for me.

Who doesn't love puppies? I sometimes distrust people who dislike dogs. I should have heeded this red flag during my speed dating days. In fact, if I ever date again, that will be a preliminary candidate screening question.

Becoming an empty-nester was a difficult transition for me. Having my kids grow up and become independent was not easy for me either, even though that is the point of good parenting. I have a need to nurture someone. For a while, I fulfilled this need years ago by fostering newborn babies awaiting adoption, which was a beautiful and humbling experience. I am honored to be a part of one of my former foster children's lives to this day.

My current working situation does not allow me to foster babies. Nor does my need for sleep. So I adopted a dog from Lab Rescue, and signed up to foster dogs awaiting adoption.

According to the American Society for the Prevention of Cruelty to Animals, approximately 6.5 million animals enter U.S. shelters every year, and approximately 1.5 million of those are euthanized.[18] There is a great need for animals to be adopted by loving owners.

Dogs can be good teachers. They make us play and exercise with them. They make us smile and laugh. They remind us to stretch. They are empathic and full of unconditional love. They are trusting and observant. I just added a book of essays regarding dogs as spiritual teachers to my reading list.[19] And I love the aspirational plaque my sponsor has on display: "Be the person your dog thinks you are."

Studies show that petting an animal can lower blood pressure. The beneficial cardiovascular effect of talking to and petting dogs has been documented, even by the National Institutes of Health.[20] Anecdotally, I certainly agree with the finding.

I have met several people who have therapy dogs who accompany them everywhere. Veterans with post-traumatic stress disorder are using therapy dogs with increasing frequency. A man in my neighborhood lost 20 pounds simply by adding rigorous dog walks to his daily routine. Perhaps having pets as we enter older age would benefit everyone.

I was not used to being alone. Having my dog with me—yes, I allow him to sleep in my bed—really gives me comfort. He loves me unconditionally and showers, eh, slobbers me with kisses. He makes me feel needed and very much alive.

The early puppy days can be challenging, of course. Maybe a cat would be less time-consuming, but still bring you needed benefits. Cats can be left alone longer.

I think God made puppies so adorable because they can be exasperating in their chewing of things around the house, high-energy antics, and not being able to control their peeing. But the trade-off is definitely worth it.

Now that arthritis has weakened my knees, I do not run very often. But boy does my dog love to walk! So not only am I bringing him joy when I take him out on walks, but I increase my physical activity. I have not completely dropped my multitasking habit. I am a recovering multitasker who is striving to be fully present in all I do.

Do you have an animal? Can you lend your time to foster one, to see if having a pet would enhance your life as it has mine? I am registered with a foster dog group that needs foster homes even for one night at a time (for when the dogs are transported to the Washington area before being adopted at their weekly adoption events).

27. Back in the Saddle

Riding a horse is not a gentle hobby, to be picked up and laid down like a game of Solitaire. It is a grand passion.

—Ralph Waldo Emerson

I am pretty much a city kid, raised in Washington, D.C., and its suburbs. Horses scared me, especially when these gloriously large, muscular, imposing beasts with large teeth reared up on their hind legs. There are actually two names for psychological fear of horses: equinophobia and hippophobia. One throw from a horse could kill or seriously maim you. Christopher Reeve, aka "Superman," became a quadriplegic after being thrown from a horse. If it can happen to Superman. . . .

Equine therapy was part of the PTSD rehab at which I was treated in Tennessee. The therapists there told me that horses have an ability to sense a human's emotions. If I were able to gain my horse's trust, he would let me brush him, lead him, and even decorate him with chalk paint.

Horses that most people ride weigh more than 1,000 pounds. They have distinct personalities. They can be gentle, wild, or stubborn. They absolutely know when a rider or caretaker is afraid or lacks control.

I started riding at this institution. When I got home, I found a place from which I could take lessons. I enjoy being around horses, hugging them, and seeing the landscape from high atop these tall beings. I even learned how to do jumps on a horse (small ones). I certainly found encounters with horses to be therapeutic.

I was surprised by how much my leg muscles ached from squeezing the sides of the horse and hovering above the saddle. Riding is not passive at all. It is a form of exercise that left me sweating from the exertion.

Riding atop a horse also gives me a different perspective on the world. I can see more new landscapes on the back of a horse and things both high and low that I may not otherwise notice on foot. Being silently in sync with this massive creature while exploring vast swaths of nature is an experience like no other.

I have heard that courage means walking through fear. Fear holds us back from so many things. I realized after entering rehab how many of my actions were governed by fear. Many people are afraid of gay people or people of color because they have no experience with them. Prejudice often is dissipated when people come to know one another. And my fear of horses dissipated by acclimating to them.

I also used Cognitive Behavioral Therapy (CBT)[21] and Dialectical Behavior Therapy (DBT)[22] skills to conquer my fears of many things, including horses. A therapist helped me learn how to challenge my inaccurate or negative thinking so that I can see situations more clearly and respond more effectively. I changed my interior dialogue about many things and learned how to regulate my emotions via CBT. I use a version of it on people close to me when they are upset or afraid. I ask them, "What is the worst that could happen?" and "Is all of that true, or are you 'awfulizing' the situation?"

We definitely build confidence and character by doing things that scare us. I am no longer fearful of horses and enjoy the physicality of riding when I can. I honestly did not believe riding could be a calorie-burning activity before I tried it, but it is. And it may be one of the few exercises that tones one's inner thighs.

I have seen challenges exhorting people to do one thing every day that scares them. Tall order, but perhaps I will. What is the worst that could happen?

28. Floating

When I stop struggling, I float.

—Anonymous

What would it be like to return to the womb, I wonder? I found something that is as close to what I can imagine that would feel like: Flotation therapy, which involves floating in warm, heavily salted water in a float tank.

Popular for years in Europe and on the West Coast of the United States, floating is starting to catch on in places along the East Coast. In 2011, there were 85 float centers in the United States, and now there are more than 250.[23] Sensory isolation in a flotation tank is a method known for inducing deep relaxation, boosting creativity, and easing body aches and pains.[24]

"Sensory deprivation chambers" were developed by scientists at the National Institutes of Mental Health in the 1950s who were studying effects of such deprivation on the brain. A 1980 science fiction/horror movie, *Altered States*, that involved sensory deprivation chambers probably set back the chambers' gaining any following in America around that time.

It was later found that flotation therapy can help with stress, addiction, fibromyalgia, ADHD, and autism spectrum disorders, among other maladies.[25] Awareness of the beneficial effects are spreading. High-performance athletes such as NBA star Steph Curry are becoming devotees,[26] which has a trickle-down effect in the general population.

A typical flotation tank contains 12 inches of body-temperature sterile water and more than 800 pounds of medical-grade Epsom salts to ensure that anyone can float. The tank I used was approximately eight feet by four feet.

Hope Floats was the first flotation studio to open in the Washington metropolitan area.[27] Its welcoming, soothing, spalike atmosphere eased my initial apprehension. Nevertheless, for the first few minutes, I was hesitant to close the door to the tank. I quickly got over my mild claustrophobia and closed the door. One can choose at the studio to listen to soft classical music or nothing at all. I tried both.

Inside the tank, I felt weightless. I could not sink, even if I wanted to do so. I actually fell asleep. When I woke up, I felt refreshed and light. I felt clearheaded, and as if I had slept for a solid eight hours.

It was cool. It was weird. I was not sure I would enjoy it, but I found it to be deeply relaxing. It eased the muscular pains I had before entering the tank and put my mind at ease. It felt like a mega-meditation and was like a mind/body reset. It was an experience I definitely will repeat. It's like a 60-minute retreat to a galaxy far, far away.

· 9 ·

Spiritual Endeavors

$\mathscr{A}$s primary caretakers for most of our child-bearing years, many of us neglected our spiritual and emotional health. Or maybe we were too busy building our careers. It is not too late to nurture growth in this area, especially now that family obligations may have receded somewhat.

There are many easily accessible spiritual teachers. Some that I follow online and respect greatly are Tara Brach, Jack Kornfield, Pema Chodron, and Brene Brown.

It took me half of my life to understand the difference between religion and spirituality. People in recovery frequently say, "Religion is for people who are afraid of going to hell; spirituality is for people who have already been there." There is a place for both in my life. I take what feeds me from organized religion and have expanded the sources that enrich my spirituality.

Now, with life experience gleaned over five decades, my spirituality has more rich soil from which to bloom. As does yours. Exploring and expanding my spirituality was a huge gift to myself that enhanced every aspect of my life. And there are many ways to experience it.

29. Excavating My Inner Wild Woman

> *You were wild once. Don't let them tame you.*
>
> —Isadora Duncan

I turned 50 and decided to run naked in the woods. I do not think there is a single woman from my "past" life who would believe I spent a retreat in the woods with a group of women I did not know, part of which involved dancing naked around a campfire howling "pussy power" at the moon. If you

95

had told me, before I turned 50, that I would be doing this, I'd have been incredulous.

The name of the retreat intrigued me. "Women of the Wild." I longed to be a Woman of the Wild. I had spent too much time holed up in a little box I believed society—and especially my straight-laced, steady, appropriate husband—wanted me to stay in. This cradle-Catholic was raised believing that anything wild, lewd, of-the-flesh (unless solely for procreation), led to infernal damnation. We were exhorted to cover our heads, shoulders, and knees while in church. I was done covering who I really was. I did not want to allow fear to govern my decisions any longer. Thus, I shed my comfort zone, pushing away any lingering wary thoughts, as my car climbed the mountains into Appalachia, into the woods and away from modern plumbing.

The retreat organizer lived near Gallaudet University, a liberal arts institution for deaf and hard-of-hearing students, and arranged for the gathering to be completely accessible, with interpreters fully fluent in American Sign Language (ASL). Initially, I felt self-conscious when talking with the deaf participants. Do I look at the interpreter? Do I look at the woman with whom I was speaking, who was looking alternatively at me and then the interpreter? What happened over the course of the retreat was a gradual easing of the hearing "barrier." We learned how to adapt and leaned in to one another. We all learned the difference between the ASL sign for "vagina" and how that sign differed from that for "pussy." We took an audacious group photo celebrating this piece of education. I no longer take for granted the facility (albeit diminishing) I still enjoy with all of my senses.

There also were lesbian and trans women present. We were of all ages, though the group skewed a bit younger than my demographic. While dancing naked around the campfire, I showed the youngsters what "elephant" skin looks like on the belly of a women who gained too much weight in pregnancy. They smiled and said I was beautiful. Perhaps I was and perhaps I was not. The point was that we were and are beautiful, just as we are. The energy and vibration we created together was dazzling, palpable, and intrepid.

We danced fully clothed as well. During open mic night, we got a "twerking" lesson from a belly dancing instructor. My half-century-old body betrayed my ambition as I struggled to keep up with the seductive moves. No matter. We laughed together and I felt a sense of freedom in my soul. Or was it freedom in my haltingly shaking pelvis that refused to contort like those of the young women? As we moved to the pulsing music that our deaf sisters felt in their bones, no one cared how they looked. When was the last time I was in a room with dozens of women who did not care one iota how they looked?

How much time I had wasted caring about my appearance! The shame from my First Communion at age seven being the only girl not dressed in white was etched into my psyche. Had my immigrant mother not known how to dress me for this occasion? Did my custodial father fail to get the memo? I still cannot look at photos from that day without feeling blood rush to my face, or at least sadness for that seven-year-old girl.

A preoccupation with being dressed appropriately for the occasion entered my public persona as the result of this and other shaming life experiences. I remember not feeling that I had the right clothes when I arrived at college. It was the 1980s, and preppiness was de rigeur at that New England gothic-spired school. I had come from a Catholic girls' high school, where we wore uniforms every day and fashion was downplayed in my friend group. I remember feeling judged and stared at by my wealthier college classmates.

At the country club we joined, I was mistaken for a server. I was painfully aware of the dress code and disappointed that my armor had not sufficed. At the large Washington, D.C., law firm where I first practiced after graduation, I was mistaken for a secretary. There is, of course, nothing wrong with servers or secretaries. I have been both. But assumptions people made, based on my appearance, stung.

Such baggage led to some stifling behavior on my part. We lived in an affluent neighborhood for a couple decades, where I would not even go outside for a run unless I was in color-coordinated attire. And it was usually high-end Lululemon brand, or the like. Now, I dress for comfort, especially while exercising. And I live in an area where people seem not to regard clothing as much beyond functional.

Does caring less about what others think come from a healthy self-esteem, borne from nurturing parents and a supportive upbringing? Does it come from maturing with sheer force of years of experience on this planet? Who knows? It is probably very case-specific. For this person in long-term recovery, it came from internalizing the sentiment that "What other people think of me is none of my business." And even if it were, it is largely out of my control.

The rain at the Wild retreat did not dampen our spirits, but rather magnified the earthy smells during our nature walks and movement between geodomes and our cabins. Everything green was glittering with moisture. It smelled loamy. I felt the soil give as I stepped into the woods, as my resistance slowly gave in.

I had a transforming experience sitting upon a rock that jutted over a river's rushing water. All sounds were drowned out, save for the river current's music. I was able to sit still with my eyes closed, attempting to empty my mind, and meditated for the longest period to date. My mind's eye conjured up the image of a phoenix behind my lids. Images came and went. I listened for my Higher Power to speak to me in some way.

I opened my eyes and gazed at the river's rocks. Most were smooth; some were still jagged. "Stop fighting, and let the river of life smooth your edges," a spirit seemed to say.

There were yoga, meditation, and "soulspeak" workshops at the retreat; sessions on unhealthy body images; and instruction on how to manifest our intentions and create our own abundance. One sublime orator shot verbal sugar through our veins, as we listened with rapt attention to her compelling words. We learned the gift of "holding space" for people we love, but cannot reach. When I hear negative thoughts from others or in my head, I learned from a wise woman, Malka Roth, now to respond with, "Return to sender, with love and consciousness," until I can release the negativity. One poet led me to a place where I was able to see myself as my own soul mate. When I shared this with her after her presentation, we both wept.

We practiced healing modalities on one another and ate vegetarian, "clean" food. I enjoyed a body massage in a makeshift studio with cloth walls that opened to the rushing river. During the closing ceremony, we took turns standing in the middle of the circle and receiving positive energy from the outstretched hands of the others who were reaching toward the woman in the center. We sealed our intentions to attract positivity and tend carefully to our dreams.

The retreat included empaths, shamans, yogis, and seekers of many kinds. Women shared their deep pain during the weekend. We were so opened up and raw following the sharing that took place, that I happily wore a red hat upon my return to civilization, being told that this would protect my Crown Chakra, which represents our ability to be fully connected spiritually—one of several spiritual self-defense tactics to which I was exposed. New to me. Why not embrace these concepts previously foreign to me? Who is to say traditional Western religions are right and Buddhists are wrong? I can now find my Higher Power anywhere. I believe we are all talking to and seeking the same God, no matter what we call Her or Him and how we approach the Spirit.

I still smile when I think about the long weekend in the woods with this amazing group of soul sisters—free of judgment, inclusive, international, authentic, open-hearted, magical women. I allowed myself the spiritual expansion I had dreamed of for years. I am working hard to dismantle the yoke of shame and fear I have carried for so long. I am banishing the word "should" from my vocabulary, in a quest to cease from "shoulding" all over myself. I am learning to love out loud, accepting life as it comes, and letting the rough edges of my life heal with the gliding water of experience that now includes the Women of the Wild.

I have adopted as my mantra a meditation Malka shared with us that was adapted from a writing of Ram Dass. After solitary meditation in the woods, she had us come together and consider picturing the world as a forest. Notice how some trees grow straight and tall, nourished by sunlight, while others bend this way and that, struggling to reach some sun above. Some trees bend and break with weight foisted upon them or weakness within, that we cannot see. So, too, are people around us like the trees. Some have easily received what they needed to thrive. Some worked hard to get what they needed, and some could not bear their circumstances. If we think of our fellows in these terms, it is much easier to practice more kindness toward all.

Remembering this metaphor for regarding others in the world has allowed me to grow in compassion toward those with whom I come in contact. I was surrounded by such love at this retreat. I pray you, too, can find a community or retreat where you can let go, expand your mind, and allow epiphanies like those I had at Women of the Wild dance in your consciousness.

30. Getting Off the Hamster Wheel

> *My religion is very simple. My religion is kindness.*
>
> —The Dalai Lama

Meditation, or centering prayer, as it is called in some Catholic circles, has gone mainstream. It has changed my life in subtle, yet noticeable ways. I no longer wrestle so much with life and fill my days with incessant doing. I slow down. I savor.

The benefits of meditation, such as stress reduction, have been widely touted. It can be an antidote to anxiety because it causes one to be present. If I am not worrying about the future or fretting about the past, I am able to be fully present. I can ground myself in the sounds and sensations I am experiencing right now.

Meditation centers have sprung up around the country. Just Meditate, in Bethesda, Maryland, is a favorite of mine, as is the Shambhala Center in Washington, D.C. Sometimes meditating in a group enables me to practice for longer periods of time and to practice meditation regularly. Gifted meditation leader Tara Brach gives weekly dharma talks in the Washington area, attended each week by hundreds of people. Her talks are recorded for online viewing.[1] Meditation retreats have gained popularity, as well.[2]

It is easy to find guided meditations online. There are dozens of apps for meditating.[3] I sometimes listen to guided meditations when stuck in traffic. They soothe me and reset my mood. Meditation can be very simple, however, with nothing more than focusing on one's own breath.

Sometimes I enhance my own practice with candlelight or aromatherapy. Meditating in a warm bath also is a lovely self-caring ritual.

Catholics call the meditation they practice centering prayer. Meditation is akin to listening for what God has to say. Although a cradle Catholic, I did not learn about centering prayer until I joined a mothers' prayer group at my church.

I was raised Roman Catholic and attended Catholic schools from first grade through college. I did not know anyone well who was not Catholic until age 18 or so. Other faith traditions were foreign to me. I remember being slightly afraid of the Mormons who would come around occasionally proselytizing door to door in our neighborhood. Fear like mine is often based on ignorance.

The Catholicism of my youth was punitive and oppressive. It was filled with guilt-inducing directives. But somehow it fed me. I now know that many children of alcoholics, like me, have inappropriate guilt in response to their parent's volatile behavior and rage. Guilt and shame are corrosive. They are something that can be released, however, if we become willing.

As I got older, I disagreed with what I considered to be the man-made mistakes in the Catholic church, such as the prohibition of birth control, lack of female clergy, condemnation of certain healing modalities as sinful superstition, and teachings on homosexuals. I believe that churches often set a high bar, knowing that humans are prone to error but need some goals toward which they can aspire. Now I take what feeds me—like the familiar prayers, ritual, and the Beatitudes—and leave the rest. I'm a cafeteria Catholic.

I explored various faith traditions and tried different churches. I have come to believe that there are many different names for our Higher Power that I choose to call God, and that there is no one right way to honor and pray to Him or Her. Actually, God is likely to not be any gender.

My very traditional ex-husband ridiculed me for some of my spiritual explorations, asking if he might come home and find me sacrificing chickens in the backyard one day. My daughter seemed to like my ventures in woo-woo land. She once said I reminded her of the socialite business mogul in the award-winning television show *Grace and Frankie*[4] before my spiritual transformation, and the hippie-dippie character afterward.

I attended services at a synagogue, a bible church, a Southern Baptist church, and a nondenominational center for spiritual development. I visited monasteries and experienced spiritual cleansing in a sweat lodge. I engaged in family constellation circles. I attended a weekly dharma talk and meditation, and tried a meditation studio. I opened my mind to different levels and methods of practicing spirituality. I learned about animal spirits and other Native American forms of spirituality.

At first, I had to shed the Catholic notion that it is a sin to worship "false gods" by engaging in superstition. Some Catholics believe that anything outside the Catholic catechism is verboten. Believing in horoscopes is considered a sin among some Catholics. I once confessed to a priest that I had gone to a clairvoyant. He forgave me, but directed me to sin no more.

I joined a Unitarian Universalist church. Unitarian Universalism is a liberal religion born of the Jewish and Christian traditions, but with a broad belief that personal experience, conscience, and reason should be the final authorities in religion. I was drawn to their inclusiveness and social justice work. Their slogan of "deeds, not creeds," attracted me. They are guided by seven principles:

—The inherent worth and dignity of every person
—Justice, equity and compassion in human relations
—Acceptance of one another and encouragement to spiritual growth in our congregations
—A free and responsible search for truth and meaning
—The right of conscience and the use of the democratic process within our congregations and in society at large
—The goal of world community with peace, liberty, and justice for all
—Respect for the interdependent web of all existence of which we are a part[5]

Hard for me to argue with these tenets.

Several coincidences happened in short order to convince me that I was being led to this church, though I no longer believe in coincidences per se. My beloved grandmother had joined a Unitarian church and is buried on the grounds of one. One of my closest friends from my Jesuit university took me to his church when I visited him in Boston and he happened to be on the Unitarian Universalist church's board there. I also had moved to a neighborhood that had a Unitarian Universalist church within walking distance and had attended dharma talks there. I saw friends—even some from my Catholic church nearby—the first time I attended a UU service at the church I joined.

Meditation is part of the Unitarian Sunday services. Meditation, however, need not be formal. It can be as simple as a deep breath before speaking or acting. Practicing the pause has saved me a great deal of pain. A working acronym for my life is WAIT: Why Am I Talking?—a big step for this previously unedited speaker.

It is a form of prayer for me. Praying, for me, had mostly been asking God for something. Meditation is listening for what God has to say. It helps me clear my mind and become grounded in the present. Sometimes, I picture a sailboat crossing on the horizon. My thoughts get "put" in the sailboat, so I can let go of them. Or, I picture a blackboard. I mentally write the racing thoughts onto the blackboard, then erase them. I take a break from the mental noise in my head.

A sea change for me spiritually was asking God what His will for me is, as opposed to asking for Him or Her to allow things to go my way. "Your will, not mine, be done."

I meditate in many different places. I attend meditation workshops and have gone to a salt cave to meditate. I have meditated atop the red rocks of Sedona, where I could sense the vibrations of the energy vortex there. I can meditate while walking. I really enjoy meditating while walking in a labyrinth, and have considered making one with stones in my backyard. They can be found in churches and parks, as an aid to entering a contemplative state.

Yoga is a meditation of movement. I can do five deep breaths at work or while stuck in traffic to bring my blood pressure down. There are a multitude of guided meditations online. Meditation is something that can be practiced at many times in one's day and in many places. Even pausing before I speak or react to something is a form of meditation.

Part of meditation for me is dropping the rock (i.e., releasing whatever it is that is holding me down). What is your rock? One of mine was being a people-pleaser and caring deeply about what others thought of me. I used to fret about what I would wear, for instance. I largely let go of that. I used to walk into a room and desperately hope everyone liked me. Now, I enter a room and hope I like them, or at least that I can relate to someone in the room.

In the 12-step meetings, we say we get a daily reprieve from our addictions, contingent on the maintenance of our spiritual condition.[6] Meditation is a large part of my spiritual maintenance. It changes my view of the world for the better. Before I take on something challenging or potentially triggering, I ask myself whether I am spiritually fit enough to undertake the event or experience in question.

I still attend mass sometimes, and am comforted by the ritual. But I believe that opening my consciousness to other ways of finding my Higher Power has strengthened me. I hope you find yours.

Quiet Down, Little One
—by Heather Markowitz
What grows there
really look closely
unspoken desires wrapping like ivy
. . . Make a clearing for it
let it unfold
guard it from naysayers. . . .
This is your dream, yours alone

What does living the life of your dreams look like for you?

31. Shamanic Wisdom

Whatever happens around you, don't take it personally. . . .
Nothing other people do is because of you. It is because of themselves.

—don Miguel Ruiz

A great deal of my journey after turning 50 has been of a spiritual nature. A book of great influence in my life is *The Four Agreements*, by Toltec shaman don Miguel Ruiz.[7] I decided to go on one of his spiritual retreats. I did not even know what a shaman was until my fifth decade, and probably would not have been open before then to going on a retreat with one.

We stayed in a small resort in the shadow of the ancient pyramids in Teotihuacan, Mexico—a UNESCO World Heritage Site. One of our shamanic sessions took place atop the largest of the pyramids. When in the presence of something so much bigger than myself, I could feel the presence of God.

Ruiz has a beatific presence. Peace radiates around him and he has many devotees. His message is of love and he seems to serve as a messenger from a Higher Power.

I had picked up Ruiz's book, *The Four Agreements*, when I was in rehab. It blew me away with the power in its simplicity. It reframed for me the way I look at the world.

Agreement number one is: "Be impeccable with your word. Speak with integrity. Say only what you mean. Avoid using the word to speak against yourself or to gossip about others. Use the power of your word in the direction of truth and love."[8] This agreement may be intuitive for most people, but was not for me. I do not wish to offend people and took pains to appeal to others—exhausting and unnecessary, for the most part, I have learned.

I also took part in gossip, as a way to elevate my fragile ego. I avoid that now. I need not contribute any more negativity to our wounded society. I find better ways to spend my time and attempt to speak only with love.

Don't take anything personally is the second agreement. "Nothing others do is because of you. What others say and do is a projection of their own reality, their own dream. When you are immune to the opinions and actions of others, you won't be the victim of needless suffering."[9] Before I respond to ugliness from another person, I try hard to remember this. I think about times I lashed out at someone not because of something they did, but because of something else that happened that did not involve them. We cannot know what is going on in other people's lives that may affect them negatively.

I have seen concrete progress using this agreement. While it still catches me off guard when someone says something mean, I am able to step back and, via my internal dialogue, not take to heart whatever was said. No one can hurt me unless I allow them to do so. I no longer give others that power.

The third agreement is: "Don't make assumptions. Find the courage to ask questions and to express what you really want. Communicate with others as clearly as you can to avoid misunderstandings, sadness and drama. With just this one agreement, you can completely transform your life."[10] The people-pleaser in me fought this agreement. But following it has increased the tranquility in my life.

In my current relationship, for example, if my boyfriend is in a sour mood, I do not jump to the conclusion that I have done something to upset him, as I may have in past relationships. I respect his space, while not taking on responsibility for how he is feeling on a given day. I also know that my very active dog can be a demanding companion, but have asked my boyfriend to tell me if he needs a break from my pup so that resentments do not build and so that I do not feel guilty when I leave my dog with him. We work hard at communicating our needs clearly and before ill feelings can erupt. We cannot read each other's minds.

The last agreement is to always do your best. "Your best is going to change from moment to moment; it will be different when you are healthy as opposed to sick. Under any circumstance, simply do your best, and you will avoid self-judgment, self-abuse, and regret."[11] This agreement helps me forgive myself. I try to remember to do the best I can with whatever my resources allow, and to hope that others are doing the best they can as well. I do not want to be an apologist for others' bad behavior, but I recognize more clearly when someone's struggles with things that have nothing to do with me color their behavior.

Each of the Ten Commandments can be found in these four agreements, yet the four agreements provided a fresh way in which to view my daily choices. There also is overlap with the teachings in my 12-step program. All are pointing me in the direction of living in grace. Before making a decision, I now ask myself, "Does this decision move me toward or away from my goal of living in grace or being the best version of myself that I can be?"

One of Ruiz's less conventional teachings is that we choose whether to love our life partners each day. At the time of the retreat, he was living with his girlfriend *and* his ex-wife, who is the mother of his children. Each day, he asks himself if he chooses to love his girlfriend that day, and she does the same. They agree they will stay together for as long as each decides to love the other. I am not sure I could subscribe to this sort of living arrangement, but I can affirmatively choose to love my significant other each day.

I incorporated this teaching into my life, in that I view love as something that must be tended to or it likely will wither away. I express love and appreciation daily to those closest to me in my life. The thought of choosing love each day strengthens it.

Are you open to the teachings of a shaman? If so, I would encourage you to check out don Miguel Ruiz's book, *The Four Agreements*. Its simple, but deep messages have changed my life for the better.

32. Good Vibrations

In order to understand the world, one has to turn away from it on occasion.

—Albert Camus[12]

I like retreats. For me, they are an opportunity to step back and reflect, away from my daily life.

I attended a spiritual retreat organized by Soul Purpose Productions, designed to raise our individual vibrations and the vibrations of our planet. It was a little bit woo-woo, and involved some clairvoyant encounters. It fed my spirit. The women seem to lack self-consciousness of the hindering type.

There is an annual holistic/psychic/yoga festival called Karmafest that Soul Purpose Productions started in 2005.[13] It attracts hundreds of different types of healers and vendors and more than 3,000 attendees from all over the mid-Atlantic. The workshops were fascinating. The topics included using your intuition gifts, spirit guides and angels, belly dancing, encountering the goddess within, using high vibrational crystals to enhance spiritual development, and many more. I particularly enjoyed the musical performances and was able to dance like no one was watching, since everyone else there appeared to be doing the same (and because I am consciously trying to practice being uninhibited). In some ways, being there felt like being transported back to the 1970s, complete with a psychedelic painted bus as a backdrop. At one point, I found myself lying in the grass, looking up at the sky simultaneously experiencing delight and relaxation, surrounded by like-minded people who also wanted to find their soul purpose. It was a far cry from my buttoned-up lawyer life in D.C.

Years ago, I took a modern dance class at a local studio. It was a disaster. I was not comfortable enough with myself to get over my feeling of awkwardness. A hip-hop session I tried was even worse. But if I took either of those classes now, I believe I could truly enjoy it, despite my lack of skill. I would likely be as poor a modern or hip-hop dancer as I was years before, but I would not care. The point is being able to let go, which is not something I easily could do prior to hitting the half-century mark. Let's drop the rock and live out loud.

Retreats abound, nowadays. There are even summer camps for adults, if that is more your style. Get away. Just for yourself. You may return with a different, more nourishing outlook.

33. Healing Self, Healing Others

Each of us has a unique part to play in the healing of the world.

—Marianne Williamson[14]

A few years ago, I would not have been open to the practice of Reiki. Reiki is healing that involves channeling energy to activate the natural healing processes of the subject's body and restore physical and emotional well-being. Both Reiki and other healing modalities are a regular part of my life post-50.

Reiki is becoming more available in clinical settings. "More than 60 U.S. hospitals have adopted Reiki as part of patient services, according to a UCLA study, and Reiki education is offered at 800 hospitals," reports *The Washington Post*.[15] When I was fostering babies awaiting adoption years ago, I would go to the hospital to touch the premature infants who had to remain there. Babies who do not experience human touch often fail to thrive. Maybe I was unwittingly performing Reiki many years ago with the babies in my care.

According to the International Center for Reiki Training:

> Reiki is a Japanese technique for stress reduction and relaxation that also promotes healing. It is administered by "laying on hands" and is based on the idea that an unseen "life force energy" flows through us and is what causes us to be alive. If one's "life force energy" is low, then we are more likely to get sick or feel stress, and if it is high, we are more capable of being happy and healthy.
>
> The word Reiki is made of two Japanese words—Rei which means "God's Wisdom or the Higher Power" and Ki which is "life force energy." So Reiki is actually "spiritually guided life force energy."
>
> A treatment feels like a wonderful glowing radiance that flows through and around you. Reiki treats the whole person including body, emotions, mind and spirit creating many beneficial effects that include relaxation and feelings of peace, security and well-being. Many have reported miraculous results.
>
> Reiki is a simple, natural and safe method of spiritual healing and self-improvement that everyone can use. It has been effective in helping virtually every known illness and malady and always creates a beneficial effect. It also works in conjunction with all other medical or therapeutic techniques to relieve side effects and promote recovery.[16]

I was dubious at first, but became a believer as I allowed myself to be more open to new ways of thinking and released myself from the social contracts in my past. I learned how to do Reiki for healing myself and others, including my dog.

My dog broke his leg as a puppy. After a rigorous fetch-the-ball session and when it is raining, he limps on that leg. After I massage his leg and perform some Reiki on it, he seems to be able to put more weight on his leg. He certainly likes the attention from me.

I made a little sign out of driftwood I found on the beach that says, "Good vibrations only." Reiki raises my vibrational energy. If I believe it to be so, it is—at least for me. Perhaps it is only a psychological effect. The mind-body connection has been studied and publicized.[17] So if Reiki affects me positively, I welcome it. I did not have a good experience trying acupuncture, though I know many people who have found it helpful. We each have the ability to find what feeds us. If we never try, we will never know.

There are many layers to Reiki practice, and I know I only have scratched the surface. Reikiinfinitehealer.com has been a helpful resource for me to learn more about Reiki's healing properties and how to use it in my life. This website offers free courses on various levels of Reiki.

Have you ever tried a Reiki session? There are Reiki practitioners throughout the United States now, as well as Reiki training centers. Many yoga studios offer Reiki training. Such training also is prevalent online and in eBooks. What do you have to lose by trying a session?

34. Random Acts of Kindness

Never worry about numbers. Help one person at a time, and always start with the person nearest you.

—Mother Teresa

I am somewhat ashamed to admit that I often did things for others because I wanted them to like me. I believe now that that need arose from not liking myself. I twistedly believed that if others liked me, the self-hatred within would dissipate.

Now I practice random and anonymous acts of kindness more often. I learned to give without needing anyone to know or thank me. I have encouraged my children to at least do this on Easter, since we are not typically together at Easter anymore and it is a positive way to share in the blessedness of the day.

I do enjoy demonstrating love through my cooking food for people. The difference is that pre-50, I wanted people to think I was like Martha F★★★★★★ Stewart via my elaborate creations and carefully crafted presentations. I used to follow recipes meticulously, without trusting my tastes or instincts. No longer.

I also engage in pro bono legal work. The sad fact is that a large percentage of our population cannot afford lawyers. Our country's legal system provides attorneys at no cost only in criminal cases in which a defendant cannot afford one. Frequently, a civil problem a person is having can be solved with one letter from a lawyer. I do what I can.

Another healing practice I try to follow now is never gossiping and steering conversations away from gossip. I attempt to adhere to Eleanor Roosevelt's proscription that "great minds discuss ideas; average minds discuss events; small minds discuss people." I try to keep my discourse infused with positivity.

What skills can you share? Anyone can provide words of encouragement. Spreading kindness does not have to be complicated.

A couple of my friends volunteer teaching English to those for whom English is not their native language. Some of my friends started giving circles to pool money to help individuals and nonprofits in need. One of these giving circles, "Womenade," gives small gifts to help individuals get to medical appointments, or funds for security deposits so they can move into subsidized housing, or even to get dentures so a person can more easily secure employment. It is not difficult to start one's own giving circle. Womenade has a how-to section on its website.[18] I held a one-time pot luck supper where each attendee brought a check for whatever amount they chose and a dish to share. It was a small effort with a real impact on people's lives. With our funds, a neighbor who is a volunteer doctor at a homeless shelter was able to help individuals obtain lifesaving prescription medicine, bus fares to job interviews, and down payments on low-income housing units.

We all can at least strive to make this world a bit better by sharing our time, talent, and treasure with others. There is a globally recognized World Kindness Day each year on November 13, which was started ten years ago by a collection of humanitarian groups under the World Kindness Movement umbrella group.[19] The World Kindness Movement seeks "to inspire individuals toward greater kindness and to connect nations to create a kinder world." I certainly want to be part of that, especially in the current political climate in which greater and more violent hatred has surfaced. If we all do our part in practicing kindness, we can elevate our society and ensure a better environment for future generations.

35. Higher Power

> *It was clear to me, as I glanced back over my earlier life, that a loving Providence watched over me, that all was directed for me by a higher power.*

—Hans Christian Andersen

Trusting in my Higher Power came with various degrees of difficulty for me. The hardest part for me was trusting that my children have their own Higher Power, which is not me.

I would die for my children. When they were little, I could largely protect them from harm. They grew into responsible adults and yet I find myself infantilizing them with my mama bear tendencies. I do tell them every day (via text, mostly) that I love them, because I will never know when my last day will be.

My daughter calls me every weekend, which I so appreciate. My son receives an allowance from me. If I do not hear his voice via a phone call, he does not get his allowance. If I did not employ this carrot approach, I doubt I would hear from him.

Instead of futile attempts to control my adult children's lives, I have learned to pray instead of attempting to fix things. I "hold a place" for them in my consciousness and send them positive energy. I practice the pause when talking to them and, through this, generally get to learn more about their lives.

I still worry about my adult children, and probably always will, but I try harder to remember that whatever happens is not in my control. They each live in cities far from mine. One is traveling around Asia; the other is in a theater conservatory in the Northeast. I think about them every day and have worked hard to consciously shift my thinking from needless worry to trust in my Higher Power. I strive to consider my life as a symphony and not let any one part of it get too loud in my consciousness.

I have family members and close friends who are alcoholics, and I experience profound sadness when they hurt themselves with their addiction. My 12-step program tells me that I cannot help them until they are ready to seek help. They must reach their own "bottom." Watching someone I love on their way to their bottom without doing anything—detaching with love—is the hardest thing I have ever done. I pray every day that those bottoms are not death. I have lost many friends to this disease.

Have you been successful at letting go? I know that worry is a waste of energy and has deleterious effects on my health. But as we say in recovery, we strive for progress, not perfection. And I am moving in the right direction.

> *If a problem is fixable, if a situation is such that you can do something about it, then there is no need to worry. If it's not fixable, then there is no help in worrying. There is no benefit in worrying whatsoever.*
>
> —The Dalai Lama

36. Raising My Spirit

> *You are a spiritual being having a human experience.*
> *You're not a human being having a spiritual experience.*
>
> —Deepak Chopra

"Do you have a photograph of yourself at age seven?" a spiritual advisor who had been recommended to me asked. I froze. "Why?" I stammered.

"I am feeling something traumatic that happened to you when you were seven years old. You need to nurture and forgive that little girl. Having a photograph of yourself at that age in a place you will often see it will help you heal." I marveled at her skills as the tears rolled down my cheeks.

At age seven, I was inappropriately fondled by someone close to our family. It happened more than once. It was confusing and I did not know what to do about it. I knew it was inappropriate, because it was done surreptitiously. But I did not tell anyone for almost two decades.

My spiritual advisor intuitively knew what had happened and helped me heal. I keep the childhood photo on my desk.

My spiritual advisor and I worked together mostly by phone because of the distance between us. Initially, the advisor's ability to know what was bothering me without my telling her was chilling, but it became comforting and helpful.

My advisor also supplied me with insights on parenting my individual children, in ways I do not believe I could have found without her. She was instantly in tune with their personalities, without ever having met them. She even helped me develop scripts I used for a couple of challenging conversations I needed to have with loved ones.

She helped me trust myself more. I slowly have learned to trust my gut instinct. Many in this field say that we all have intuitive powers that are especially strong when we are children, which then dissipate if they are not exercised and honed. Toltec Shaman and bestselling author don Miguel Ruiz[20] maintains that we allow the world to impose judgment into our psyches and, as a result, lose some of the gifts with which we are born, such as powerful intuition and a sense of wonder about the world.

Another friend of mine, Jessica Epperson-Lusty, describes the need to trust our own inner guidance:

> If we do not become conscious of what distorts our perception of our circumstances and our relationship with our intuitive guidance, we continue being led by external forces that may not support the expression of our authentic gifts, our soul's fulfillment, and evolution in this life.[21]

Jessica uses a holistic approach to provide individuals with guidance along their paths of personal empowerment and enlightenment. She hosts workshops, retreats, yoga sessions, and JourneyDance events in her healing pursuits. I so admire her work in helping others evolve, and hope to attend one of her retreats in the near future.

I am, I know, lucky that my spiritual advisor was not a charlatan. It is supremely important to get personal recommendations before embarking on a path involving a spiritual advisor. I once met a tarot card reader in Georgetown who tried to get me to pay her thousands of dollars to help heal my bloodline. I was in such a bad place that I considered it for a long time before declining.

There are many types of spiritual guides. Mine calls herself, among other things, an intuitive consultant. She says, "As an intuitive consultant, energy worker, healer, and spiritual development teacher, I use my (clairaudient, claircognizant, clairsentient, and clairvoyant) abilities to discern the information I receive. I ask to serve as a healing instrument for the highest and best good of each client. I 'tune in' and the authentic journey begins."[22]

In the Catholic church, and other places of worship, there are spiritual directors available. This is, of course, a different approach, but also helpful to many.

My spiritual advisor has given workshops about harnessing our personal power, which I have been glad to attend. She also has opened my mind to angels. She told me that whenever I see a feather, my guardian angel is with me. I now notice hundreds of feathers, some in unlikely places. And every time I see one, I smile. They show up seemingly when I most need the reminder of feeling protected.

I am more open to the idea of prior lives—that we are at our essence souls having human experiences, perhaps numerous times. I am open to many new possibilities.

Although it took me a while to begin working with a spiritual advisor, I admired several friends who did, long before I took the plunge. Such advisors seemed to help these friends to overcome some significant hurdles in their lives and to live in more grounded ways.

I was a bit anxious when I first called my spiritual advisor. Since she was a clairvoyant as well, I worried that she would read my mind and sense my thoughts. And the Catholic prohibition embedded in me regarding belief in the work of clairvoyants as a form of false god worship had given me pause as well. I still have skepticism but, like everything else, I take what feeds me and leave the rest.

Is seeing a spiritual advisor or spiritual director something you are open to trying? Or, if you have never consulted a counselor or therapist, would you be interested? Opening up to another person can ease our burdens and provide new dimensions of looking at our lives. Just telling someone else about anything bothering you can lighten its effect on you and make you feel that you are not alone in whatever the matter weighing on you may be.

· *10* ·

Thrill-Seeking Ventures

$\mathcal{W}$e are not dead yet! Who couldn't use a bit of excitement in their lives? Excitement helps us to remain vibrant and interesting (most importantly, perhaps, to ourselves). Remember the feeling of adrenaline coursing through your veins? It makes you stronger and faster, and makes everything seem more vivid. Maybe it is not something I want to experience every day, but bursts here and there are like cardiac revival paddle shots to my being. I consider exciting adventures to be a sort of defibrillation from mediocrity, complacency, and even despair.

I know that I am physically unable to do some of the things I could do even a decade ago, when I ran marathons. My knees sometimes hurt when climbing stairs. But I am not giving up.

Madonna is in her late 50s. Meryl Streep is in her late 60s. Cher is in her late 70s. Are they leading sedentary, staid lives? No. Why should we? We certainly do not have to. Even former president George H. W. Bush marked his 90th birthday by skydiving. I could do that! But since I do not know whether I will live to age 90, I may as well do it now.

I have many more exhilarating plans for myself, like getting my scuba certification so I can dive deeper than the shallow resort dives I have been lucky enough to try. Here are a few possible ideas for your consideration. At least they may inspire ideas that fit your unique personality.

37. Wind Therapy (Or, What It's Like to Pretend to Be a Hells Angel)

> *On a cycle the frame is gone. You're completely in contact with it all. You're **in** the scene, not just watching it anymore, and the sense of presence is overwhelming.*
>
> —Robert M. Pirsig[1]

Much to my children's horror, I learned how to ride a motorcycle and got one of my own. I told them they were welcome to do the same after they turned 50. I wanted to try something daring, and this definitely was outside of my comfort zone.

There were classes offered at the local community college and at an area Harley-Davidson dealer. You know which location I chose. There was only one other woman in the class I took. The rest of the students were burly, tough guys, and one cop in training. One guy dropped out, stomping away after he flailed off the practice course while attempting a turn.

I was shaking a little the first time I got on the bike. It was so heavy that it was hard for me to hold it steady when I came to a stop. It definitely was easier to ride than to stop or stay still on a motorcycle. These Harleys had roll bars on their sides so that, if dropped by a student, the bike would not get damaged (and our legs would not get crushed). I dropped mine twice while practicing on the course. But I proudly passed the three-day course and went straight to the Motor Vehicles Administration to get my motorcycle license. Shortly after that, I bought a small used motorcycle, a Suzuki 350. I may get a Harley after I have more experience riding.

Wind therapy. I now know what that means. Being on a motorcycle on a country road with the wind on your face and the sun at your back is therapeutic. I imagine sailing and other sports can have this effect as well.

One of my favorite authors, Ann Patchett, observed that "people are more than willing to die on motorcycles because for that moment . . . they are truly and deeply alive."[2] I have learned, however, that she does not endorse motorcycle riding, by any means.

I feel fierce and alive on a motorcycle. Being in a car has become somewhat like watching a moving television screen for me. When I get on a motorcycle, or even a bike or scooter, I smile at the unfiltered beauty around me and the sun warming my arms.

Each time I mount that rumbling 500-plus pounds of metal, it is a thrill. It feels dangerous and powerful. It *is* dangerous and powerful. There is little between you and the pavement. Every time I ride, I must remain acutely aware of the vehicles around me, knowing that many will not notice where I am on the road. I need to look ahead in the distance, at the road to avoid potholes and other hazards, and side to side for turning cars, pedestrians, and animals. One careless moment can result in maiming or death. It helps to wear bright colors to be more visible and to continually look for escape routes if another driver stops suddenly or moves into your lane. In the evening on country roads, some of my rider friends honk their horns to keep deer from jumping onto the road.

I would not have done this had my children still been dependent upon me. They always came first. But being on the downslope of my life (some call it "the third third"), I am less afraid of dying. I am more afraid of not living vibrantly and with intention. My children and my good works are my legacy. Diminishing fear is another benefit of aging.

Our society has imbued bikers with a sort of "bad boy/girl" image. Some bikers promote the mystique. Hells Angels and other outlaw motorcycle clubs still exist. They wear patches or "colors" to indicate their loyalty. The American Motorcyclist Association is credited with the comment that 99 percent of motorcyclists are law-abiding citizens, implying that the last one percent were outlaws. The outlaw clubs often wear one percent patches to celebrate this dubious distinction. I usually wear something brightly colored and thereby more visible to other drivers, thereby adding a modicum of safety.

What I have found in meeting other motorcycle enthusiasts is a nonjudgmental, brotherhood/sisterhood atmosphere. There are bikers of all ages and socioeconomic backgrounds. They wave or nod to one another on the road. Strangers on bikes frequently join up to ride together to increase their visibility on the road. They like to share ride stories. We have easy conversations with other motorcycle enthusiasts wherever we go. Harley-Davidson dealerships welcome bikers to stop in and have free coffee and sometimes other treats.

Patriotism and honoring veterans are huge in the biker community. I got tears in my eyes at the first Rolling Thunder event I attended, in which veterans were honored by thousands of bikers in downtown Washington, D.C. It was not at all what I expected. I thought the Rolling Thunder attendees would not be emotional types and had bought into the on-screen depictions of motorcycle gangs as being representative of the majority of bikers. While many bikers I meet appear unapproachable, hardened, and somewhat scary, conversations with them have revealed truly congenial people. Another batch of my assumptions dismantled.

Bikers' Week events take place all over the country. The few I have attended have been fun and low key, featuring food, music, bikes and accessories, and hilarious helmet stickers. Many of the stickers were quite bawdy. Some examples: "Horn broken. Watch for Finger." "Of course, they're real. If they were fake, they'd be bigger." "I have a lot of class; unfortunately it's all low." "For some there's therapy. For the rest of us there's [*sic*] motorcycles." "I'm not a gynecologist, but I'll take a look." I didn't say they were in good taste.

Of course, many from my "old life" still carried the societal assumptions about people who ride motorcycles. I was practicing my riding skills one day and passed a woman whose children attended my son's tony private school in D.C. I stopped to chat and said, "Yes, my kids are horrified that I got a motorcycle." In a clipped voice, she responded, "So am I." I took a look at her and felt a moment of shame. Then I vroom-vroomed and sped away. I no longer allow myself to be governed by other people's judgments. That's their baggage, not mine.

Motorcycle riding feels powerful. There are hundreds of pounds of metal being controlled by the rider with a turn of the wrist. The sound is loud (sometimes, purposefully so, to increase drivers' awareness of a motorcyclist's presence on the road nearby). The thrill is palpable. And it is cheaper than driving a car and leaves a smaller carbon footprint on Mother Earth. Parking is a breeze. At crowded venues, motorcycles often are permitted to park on the grass or in special areas close to entrances.

I have ridden on the back of a motorcycle from Washington, D.C., to Montreal. I find it meditative. I have seen so much more wildlife along the way than I otherwise would have had a chance to see. My eyes are opening wider with each new adventure.

Is motorcycle riding something you would like to try? It is less difficult than I thought it would be. It helped that I knew how to drive a car with standard transmission, so I understood some about shifting gears. Maybe learning how to drive a car with a stick shift is something that would give you a thrill. Or going off road in a jeep or on an ATV. Remember that the most dangerous risk of all is the risk of spending your life not doing what *you* want.[3]

38. Learning How to Fire

If I were to remain silent, I'd be guilty of complicity.

—Albert Einstein

I now know how to shoot a gun. A ranch I visited offered shooting lessons with six-shooter revolvers and 22-caliber rifles. I was good at hitting the target. I gained an appreciation for gun shooting as a sport, and increased my understanding of people who love guns. I do not believe in violence and do believe in gun control, but have to admit that shooting a gun is a potent experience. Really, mastering any new skill is empowering.

My learning how to shoot is a metaphor for another change in my life: I learned how to stand up for myself and for others, how to shoot back. Up to this point in my life, I have assumed a deer-in-the-headlights posture when faced with ugly remarks by another person. Momentarily stunned, I do not come up with appropriate retorts until minutes or hours later.

A gay friend, Michael Sharp, who unfortunately was accustomed to dealing with bigotry, taught me an effective way to deal with these unsettling comments. At the very least, he counsels, I could respond with a "wow" to indicate my surprise and displeasure. To drive the point home, without direct confrontation, I can ask for clarification, such as in, "You mean you think that person is stupid?" What I have observed is that, by getting the speaker to repeat the offending remark a few times, they often are embarrassed about the hatefulness they have spewed.

My son is gay, as are many of my friends and associates. An unfortunate colloquialism I have heard far too many times is, "That's so gay." This is supposed to indicate that something is unworthy of respect or is something a manly guy would not like or do. It is offensive to me, and I no longer let that comment pass without negative acknowledgment.

I also have friends with children who have Down syndrome or other disabilities. Children with Down syndrome are incapable of hatred or meanness. Those in my life who have disabilities have each made me a better person, simply for knowing them and their goodness. When someone remarks that something or someone is "retarded," and they mean to disparage the object of the comment in doing so, I call them on their misuse of the word. There are now campaigns to end the use of the "R-word," by such organizations as Best Buddies.

Words can hurt. I will do my part to raise consciousness around such barbs.

I felt radical shooting this loud, dangerous instrument, and certainly out of my element. Shooting a gun feels powerful. So does standing up for myself and others.

39. Thirty Seconds of Fame

> I'm more interested in being good than being famous.
>
> —Annie Leibovitz

I was too self-conscious to perform on stage when I was a young student, though I admired those I knew who did. I worked behind the scenes as a crew member in high school on a few plays, but wished for the courage to perform.

My son is pursuing a career in musical theater. I am blown away when I watch him step on stage and belt out a song with seeming ease and no evidence of stage fright. I would shake and sweat profusely if I had to do that. My voice would tremble.

I once accompanied him to an acting gig he had as an extra on the award-winning HBO show *VEEP*. His agent got him the job and because he was a minor at the time, I knew I would be hanging around with him all day on the set. So I asked the agent if I could be an extra on the show and she got me on the episode as well.

I learned that television production takes a great deal of time for each scene. I was surprised by the number of takes required. I enjoyed watching the excellent actor Julia Louis-Dreyfus sometimes improvise her lines with her brilliant comedic skill and timing. My son's takeaway from the experience was that he would rather perform in live theater.

I got a little thrill from seeing myself on the small screen. I next signed up as an extra on the locally filmed Netflix television series, *House of Cards*. I enjoy the show, and Kevin Spacey would sometimes entertain the extras with witty banter between takes. Because I am short (and maybe because I appear ethnically ambiguous), I frequently got put at the front of any crowd or group scene.

Friends around the country sent me messages when they saw me on the show. Many thought I had a doppelganger. "I could have sworn I just saw you on *House of Cards*," people would text me.

I also got work on a political commercial for Planned Parenthood. An adorable baby was put in my arms and I was filmed with her for the spot. Voice-over speech was added in production. A friend said she saw the ad in Las Vegas. I got a small check, a credit for my résumé, and some nice photos I could use for head shots in future submissions.

I took a brief continuing education drama class that was great fun. If I did not have to work as a lawyer to make a sustainable living, I probably would pursue more acting opportunities. There are so many local and regional theaters that can provide outlets for those of us who have an acting itch.

I now subscribe to a free newsletter that advertises work for actors and submit for jobs every once in a while. Some auditions are accepted by video.

I certainly have met a cast of characters on the sets I have visited. I do not make much money as an extra. But it is fun and stretches my comfort zone, occasionally. And the productions usually feed you. . . .

40. Skydiving

Think you can, think you can't . . . either way, you'll be right.

—Henry Ford

On my daughter's 18th birthday, she asked to go skydiving. I watched as she fell from the sky. I was pacing, sweating, and praying for her safety.

Former president George H. W. Bush went skydiving on his 90th birthday. I do not know if I will skydive from an airplane during my lifetime. Maybe when I am 60, or 70, or 80, or even 90. I did, however, want to address my fear of heights.

Some indoor skydiving places have cropped up around the Washington, D.C., area. Indoor skydiving is the simulation of true free fall conditions—like jumping out of an airplane—in a vertical wind tunnel. It feels like flying, a superpower I had dreamed of and longed for in my youth.

We were given a short bit of classroom instruction before donning the safety gear, consisting of goggles, a helmet, a jumpsuit, and earplugs for the noise. When we entered the tunnel, we were accompanied by a safety instructor who taught us how to control our bodies within the airflow. We each flew in a column of wind created by the vertical, glass-enclosed wind tunnel.

We could choose to fly only in the lower part of the tunnel or 30 feet higher in the upper part of the chamber. I am proud to say that I chose the latter.

Indoor skydiving gets its name from the thrill-seeking sport of skydiving, but the similarities between the two are actually very few. A vertical wind tunnel creates the needed vertical wind flow for indoor skydiving. This simulates the conditions found in free fall without the need to jump from a great height. Because the wind tunnel environment is very controlled compared to the traditional free fall of a skydive, a wider range of flyers can take part in the experience.

An advantage of indoor skydiving is that outdoor skydiving is completely dependent on the weather. Another is that indoor skydiving lasts longer. An average skydive from 13,000 feet lasts less than one minute. Typical indoor skydiving flights last between two and five minutes, which gives people more time to learn how to control their flying. Indoor skydiving has become a worldwide recognized sport. Our instructor treated us to a demonstration of some wild tricks in the wind tunnel. I can see that, with practice, indoor skydiving could be addictive because it causes such an adrenaline rush.

I thought I would be afraid, being so high in the air. But I was not, in this situation. Flying felt liberating, like breaking through another dimension. I loved it.

Indoor Skydiving Source maintains a list of all indoor skydiving facilities throughout the world.[4] Anyone over age five can do indoor skydiving. I am now open to trying outdoor skydiving in the future. Are you ready for this type of challenge?

41. Inked

> *Show me a man with a tattoo and I'll show you a man with an interesting past.*

—Jack London, 1883

Sometimes I still cannot believe I got a tattoo. Sometimes, when I see it, it catches me by surprise. "What is that?" my mind asks. "Did I really do that?"

When I was growing up, tattoos were extremely radical. They were primarily associated with sailors and misfits. Not so much nowadays, with the likes of Angelina Jolie, Halle Berry, Jennifer Aniston, and numerous professional athletes sporting them. But I felt a bit of a bad girl thrill when I was getting mine.

I remember being a bit shocked when one of my former law school roommate got a large phoenix tattooed on her back. She, like me, emerged later in life from a troubled past. Her phoenix is symbolic of her journey. I now understand and respect her choice.

Getting the tattoo did not hurt. Nothing really hurts very much after childbirth, I suppose. It felt more like scratching. The tattoo artist said the big tough-looking guys are usually the biggest babies about the process.

I got the tattoo on the Venice Beach boardwalk. I made sure clean needles were used, since I had been told of the disease hazards of unsterile needles.

Because my job involves gaining credibility with some fairly conservative types—like judges—I got my tattoo on my wrist where it can be covered completely by a watchband. Maybe I will get to a point where I never hide it.

I sometimes wonder what it will look like when my skin loses elasticity. I have seen tattoos on wrinkled skin that are not appealing. I have a friend who makes a lot of money removing tattoos.

Actor Nicolas Cage is credited with saying that his tattoos were outward symbols of inward change. Prehistoric cultures used tattoos as protection charms, good luck amulets, faith symbols, or pure decoration.[5] I guess I did mine for all of these reasons.

Aside from feeling a bit rebellious, I got a tattoo on my wrist with a word meaningful to me, to remind me how I want to live my life: "Grace." Grace means several things to me: "But for the grace of God," grace of the Holy Spirit, living in grace and not in fear, grace to surrender, and having the grace to accept God's will, among several others.

Maybe I did not have to emblazon something permanently onto my body. I already wear jewelry that carries messages for me such as "Slow down" and "I am enough." Some people wear temporary tattoos for a while before getting real ones, to see if they like them.[6] I did that, initially. And I have put messages on my cell phone home screen, like "This day," as in "Give us this day our daily bread," from the "Our Father" prayer. When I say that prayer now, I stress the words "this day." I feel more and more mortal as I age and want to remember to relish each day that I have been given.

One disadvantage to tattoos: I lost credibility in telling my young adult children why they shouldn't get piercings or tattoos. Oh well. They are forging their own paths anyway. And I need to improve at letting them learn from their own mistakes.

Are there outward symbols you would like to employ to remind you of or to celebrate inward change? Of course it need not be via a tattoo. It could be jewelry. I have a ring with a Sanskrit symbol of universality on it that I wear frequently, and a bracelet on which the Serenity Prayer is engraved. It could even be a Post-it on your bathroom mirror. It is just for you, after all. But if you do go for a tattoo, at least go to a reputable tattoo artist/parlor.

· *11* ·

Lifestyle Changes

$\mathcal{F}$ifty is a good time to take stock of what is and what is not working in your life. Things do not ever have to remain the same. Even small changes, like attitudinal changes, can yield meaningful and powerful results. Why not take the time to improve the quality of your life? When you are more satisfied with yourself and your life, those around you experience positive reverberations. Put on your air mask first, so you can be of better service to others.

42. I Am Enough

The worst loneliness is not to be comfortable with yourself.

—Mark Twain

For 20 years during my marriage, I vacationed on the island of Nantucket, Massachusetts, where my then-husband's family had a big house on Main Street. Reflecting on those times, I now realize they were not much in the way of relaxation.

It was if I was exchanging one stage for another. Nantucket is like a movie set, with well-dressed, moneyed people milling about everywhere. We were yacht club members, though our family no longer owned a boat. We played tennis, ate, and socialized at the club, though it was not a place to relax for me. I felt that I always had to be "on" there—well-dressed, well-behaved, and demonstrating impeccable social graces.

Many Washingtonians vacation in Nantucket, and it is a lovely place, devoid of traffic signals, parking meters, fast food, and retail chains. For sale signs are not even permitted in front of available real estate. It is clean and much concerted land preservation effort has paid off. But I rarely enjoyed its natural beauty. I went out of my way to organize clambakes and other social events for friends and family. It was exhausting.

After turning 50, I learned about the need for rejuvenation via vacations, and the benefit of solo time. I go on yoga and spiritual retreats, and visit rural areas, to relax. I frequently seek out solitude, not socializing. I still enjoy the stimulation of exploring new places, hearing new music, and meeting people from different backgrounds. But I have learned to enjoy my own company, rather than to avoid it. I fully understand the difference between being alone and being lonely now.

I have learned the utility of downtime. I don't feel the need to entertain and put on any sort of show, like I used to do. My self-worth used to be correlated with other's reactions to my efforts. Now, however, I have learned to just be.

And I do not need other people's approval anymore, for the most part. Before I turned 50, eating alone in a restaurant would be quite uncomfortable. It isn't anymore. I cannot control what other people think and am not responsible for what they think of me. Like other alcoholics, I was "an egomaniac with an inferiority complex." Sounds like an oxymoron, but it is true on many levels. I had to take steps to remedy this feature of my character. My own judgmentalism, including toward myself, was borne out of my insecurities. We all have our own realities, and none are identical. We see what we want to see.

While I currently have a boyfriend, I will always keep my own house and independence. When I leave his company for a few days, I find that we appreciate each other even more. We each have disparate interests, but enough shared interests, to suit our desire to spend time together as well as apart. I believe that we will treat each other better if we keep our own identities and can walk away at any time. Each day we can actively choose to love each other and spend time with each other.

The greatest lesson I learned in this chapter of my life is that no one is responsible for my happiness but myself. I was continuously looking for outside people or things or situations to make me happy. But no one is perfect and, because we are all human, no relationship is perfect. As I moved from one relationship to another, I realized that I was trading one set of problems for another. The key is appreciating what is around you already, finding inner peace, and enjoying the precious present.

> There will be times when other people will disappoint us—either intentionally or because of indifference or incompetence. If we have been counting on them, their nonperformance can cause us real anger and frustration.
>
> Our growth, however, should teach us that such failures are part of life. While never losing trust in others, we must accept them as fallible people.

Their mistakes and lapses come from the human shortcomings all of us have.

Our best course is to live without expecting too much from others. They are not here to please or satisfy us. It's possible, too, that we've been unrealistic in some of our expectations and have set ourselves up for disappointments.

Our personal responsibility is to do our best even when others fall short of our expectations. At the same time, we can grow by becoming more reliable and dependable ourselves.

We cannot use another's failure as an excuse for negligence on our part.

—from *Walk in Dry Places*, by Mel B.[1]

I have traded the high-brow flavor of Nantucket for the more bucolic pace of rural Vermont when I have the chance to get away for a while. It is quiet and no one I have met there puts on any sort of airs. When I am in the Green Mountain State, specifically the Northeast Kingdom, I feel truly relaxed. I take long walks, decompress, take stock, and relish my inner peace. Solitude no longer feels lonely.

43. Seaside Sanctuary

A woman must have money and a room of her own.

—Virginia Woolf[2]

My ex-husband kept the house we shared for more than 20 years. I didn't fight him for it because I felt so guilty for the role I played in the demise of our marriage. He paid me for half of its appraised value. I wanted to live on the edge of a body of water. I quickly discovered that "on the water" real estate listings commanded double or triple the price of "water view" abodes.

I lucked into finding a little cottage in a part of Maryland near the Chesapeake Bay that I did not know existed. I looked for months for a place that was on the water, but realized that any "waterfront" listing was out of my price range. "Water view" properties were closer to my budget.

As a person with liberal views, I did not want to live in a neighborhood that was ultra-conservative. As a person of color, I sought to avoid any areas that were known to have active Ku Klux Klan.[3] A few of the listings I checked out were eliminated from consideration when I saw confederate flags displayed in the neighborhood.

My new home is an hour from D.C., my workplace, and my children's childhood home, at which they mostly want to stay during school breaks, given the proximity of their friends. Some close friends let me stay at their summer house in this neighborhood while I was house-hunting. An older couple on the street had received no offers on their cottage that had been on the market for months, and I was able to purchase their house for less than half the funds I received for half of my former marital home.

I have never before owned any house by myself. It felt like a huge milestone. I felt anchored.

I furnished my house mostly with yard sale and Goodwill store finds. eBay became my Saks Fifth Avenue. I made a wreath for my door out of driftwood I found on the beach. I saw that a neighbor had an old wooden oar as a stair banister and asked her where she got it. "Just wait for one to wash up on the beach," she said. And one did, shortly thereafter.

My house came out pretty well, in a "shabby chic" sort of way. I enjoyed the challenge of finding things, repurposing things, and making things. I slowly covered my parking area with shells I found on the beach, and framed interesting feathers and other beach finds. Almost everything can look artistic when in a frame that suits it. Every single thing in the house was something I liked—a reflection of me alone.

I even have an altar of spiritual talismans in my home. At my first rehab, the spiritual director shared with me that she had an altar at her home and if any person she dated saw it and negatively commented on it, they would not receive any more of her time. She sought the company only of people who accepted her for who she was. I longed for that outlook and confidence, and moved my attitude in that direction. I smudged my home with sage—something I learned about at rehab—to rid of any negative energy, including that which I brought in myself.

My little house is my oasis of calm. My seaside sanctuary. I left most windows uncurtained, so it is filled with light. I am able to hear and see the Chesapeake Bay and its indigenous wildlife.

After I left, my ex-husband decided to redecorate the home we had shared. He graciously gave me some of the furniture he no longer wanted. I stopped by to pick up what he had left on the back porch for me one day when he was at work. I peeked into the window and saw two men painting over the vibrant apple-green walls of our family room. "He's erasing me," I lamented, as tears streamed down my face. The painters opened the door. The older of the two said his daughter had recently divorced and he gave me a hug. He said, in a fatherly way, "Leave the furniture. It will only bring back sad memories." Practical Maria sprung into my psyche. "No, I want the furniture."

I'm glad I took it. It was all stuff I had chosen in the first place, and time is healing my sadness at the loss of my marriage.

It felt cleansing to have fewer things and to consciously live with less. I try to employ the practice of getting rid of two things for every one thing I bring into my house. It feels good to get rid of things I do not want, to make more room for what I do want, which in many instances is simplicity. Less clutter also means less to clean.

I no longer care so much about wearing what is in style and focus instead on what looks good on me and what is comfortable. Buying things second-hand makes me feel that I am doing my small part in helping improve our environment by not making an even bigger carbon footprint with my purchases of new items. Plus, at this juncture in my life, I would rather spend my money on experiences instead of things.

Maybe you already like where you live, or have no choice but to stay where you are for the time being. You can likely reclaim a corner of your dwelling just for you and things that inspire you. It can be your meditation space, your recharging space, your place to practice a pause before reacting or responding to whatever life has thrown at you. Charge your space with good energy. Consider blessing it with holy water or smudging it with burning sage. It does not have to be a big space or hard to do. I have a friend who made a closet into her own space for working or meditating. The space just needs to be dedicated to *you*, because you are worth it.

I used to equate pleasure with happiness. Now, for me, happiness is more lasting. It is contentment with life as it is. It is letting go of the results. It is finding meaning in my life. It is being grateful. A wise mentor who passed from cancer long ago told me that we must experience the valleys in order to appreciate the peaks. I finally know what she means.

44. Life by the Water

> *I'm always happy when I'm surrounded by water. . . .*
> *The ocean makes me feel really small and it makes me put my whole life into perspective . . . it humbles you and makes you feel almost like you've been baptized.*
> *I feel born again when I get out of the ocean.*
>
> —Beyoncé Knowles

I am afraid of sharks. The 1975 movie *Jaws* kept me out of the ocean for years. According to *National Geographic*, we have a one in 63 chance of dying from the flu and a one in 3,700,000 chance of being killed by a shark.[4] I did not claim that my fear was rational.

Now that I live near the water, I have overcome some of that fear. I took up paddle-boarding and kayaking. Watching the sun set from a kayak is an unparalleled experience for me. The sun glitters off the water. You sit so low that you can feel the water—almost feel a part of it—yet be cocooned in safety at the same time.

I live close to the Chesapeake Bay. I can see it from the second floor of my house. Life is slower there than in the D.C. metropolitan area. The Chesapeake Bay is the largest estuary in North America. I am surrounded by vast natural beauty and people who care deeply about the environment.

As a city slicker, I still come across animals around my new home that I cannot identify, like these small beaverlike creatures that scurry across the winding roads. And the horseshoe crabs still startle me with their Darth Vader-esque appearance. If they wash up on the beach, however, I am now able to physically direct them back into the water without trepidation.

Living near water relaxes me. There is a bridge I cross when I near my neighborhood. When I see it, I feel stress melting away. Water is picturesque and serenity-inducing. We can float on it and be caressed by it. Its rhythms can lull us; its size and power can bring perspective and humility. We cannot live without water. It is elemental.

According to NASA:

> From ancient times, explorers have "followed the water." Water's unique chemical and physical properties are essential to human survival. Without water, basic physical processes would be impossible. Cells within the human body would die. None of the essential physical functions, such as breathing, digestion, or muscle movement could take place without water.
>
> About 70 percent of the human body is made up of water and, coincidentally, more than 70 percent of Earth is covered in water. Water creates an environment that sustains and nurtures plants, animals and humans, making Earth a perfect match for life in general.[5]

Thank God for water.

It is also fun to play in water. It can bring out the child in us. My dog loves to swim and to chase the balls I throw to him on the beach and from the water's edge. It is no wonder that so many people flock to be near water during their vacation time.

I never want to take it for granted that I live near water. I am blessed to do so. I often sit on my second-floor porch with my morning coffee admiring the glittering bay. Back in the suburbs where I used to live, several friends of mine put ponds with small waterfalls in their backyards, to wonderful, relaxation-inducing effect. We are all lucky to be able to enjoy and employ the healing power of water.

My mother grew up in a nation composed of more than a thousand islands—the Philippines—and still does not know how to swim. Water, while soothing, can be dangerous, of course. I have read news reports of toddlers drowning in less than two inches of water.

I would like to learn how to boat safely, at some point. I currently know how to sail out away from the land, harnessing the power of the wind, but would have difficulty tacking back. But that's okay for now. Maybe that can be on my list of 60 after 60.

When my children were little, I had a sound machine that would lull them to sleep with the sound of ocean waves. How about a meditation employing that soothing sound? A quick YouTube search of "meditation sound of the ocean" brought up hundreds of videos/soundtracks of varying lengths. I have used one of these to drown out noise when concentrating on difficult tasks at work where the walls are thin.

If you have never tried snorkeling or, better yet, scuba diving, I encourage you to do so. Scuba diving is like visiting another world. You need not be certified to do a "resort dive" or a "discovery dive," which is a dive of less than 30 feet or so, with a short instruction session preceding. I was able to witness my children's first experience breathing under water, which was a gift. Was their response to the magnificence we saw under water as effusive as I had wanted? No. But that is okay. I have let go of expectations like that and fantasies of how things should be. I loved the experience with my children, and know they enjoyed it. I delighted in the variety of corals, giant clams, and colored fish we got to see. At one point, I was engulfed by a school of fish that formed a yellow curtain around me. It was magical.

Do you have opportunities to experience the healing, relaxing power of water? If land-locked, perhaps you can spend time floating in a pool, lake, or pond? Or even listening to the soothing sound during a meditation break?

45. Keep It Simple

Life is really simple, but we insist on making it complicated.

—Confucius

There was a time when buying a pair of Louboutin heels could bring me such pleasure. I mistook the fleeting excitement I felt when opening a Tiffany box to be happiness. American culture has many of us fooled into believing that consumption yields happiness. Money, however, does not buy joy. After our basic needs are met, there is a certain point at which having more money does not increase our ability to be happy. As one psychologist noted: "If we become less materialistic, our well-being will improve. If our well-being improves, we tend to be less materialistic."[6] Post-50, I shed the phenomenon of wanting more that had governed an earlier part of my life.

There is a growing minimalist movement in America. "Minimalism is a tool to rid yourself of life's excess in favor of focusing on what's important—so you can find happiness, fulfillment, and freedom," say documentarians and mini-malist advocates Joshua Fields Millburn and Ryan Nicodemus.[7]

I have a friend, Heather Markowitz, who is joining the Tiny House Movement—which is a brand of minimalism—and is building her very small house from the ground up.

> Simply put, [the tiny house movement] is a social movement where people are choosing to downsize the space they live in. The typical American home is around 2,600 square feet, whereas the typical small or tiny house is between 100 and 400 square feet. Tiny houses come in all shapes, sizes, and forms, but they enable simpler living in a smaller, more efficient space.[8]

Heather used GoFundMe to help raise funds and held building and painting parties to move the project along. She is environmentally and socially conscious and teaches me via her example.

I applaud people who live in tiny houses. While I am not quite ready to join this movement (for one, I would like to have my adult children stay with me when they visit), I consciously have simplified my life and live in a smaller house now. I have shed many unnecessary possessions on eBay, Craigslist, and consignment stores, and given many items to charities. I endeavor to give away two things for every one thing I bring into my home.

I am a fairly sentimental person, so sometimes it is hard for me to let go of items that hold special memories for me. I know objectively, however, that I do not need as much as I thought I needed before hitting age 50, and I am doing my children a favor by sorting through my possessions and getting rid of junk so they do not have to do so for me when I am gone.

I also am a thrifty person, so that when I cull my closet of clothing, I hear that voice saying, "You will lose the weight to fit into that again" and "That will come back into style." Seldom have those things come true in my life. But this particular dialogue continues in my head.

In the United States, we are bombarded with advertising. It is the job of an entire multimillion-dollar industry to get our attention in a multitude of ways. Some advertisers use subliminal messages to make us want to buy their products. Newspapers and magazines would go out of business if they had no advertising revenue. Ads permeate almost every aspect of American life. More people I know watch the Super Bowl commercials than the Super Bowl itself.

When I encounter an ad that makes me want to purchase something online, I put the item in my online basket and leave it there for at least a day before buying it. More often than not, after this self-imposed waiting period, I choose not to buy it after all.

Sometimes I challenge myself not to buy anything for two days, or even a week at a time. I have a friend who gave up buying anything during Lent except essentials. This practice makes me use what I have in more creative ways. I have made some surprisingly delicious pantry and leftover meals. I have put together new outfit combinations that I really liked. In this way, I have become more aware of what I consume and the distinction between want and need.

I keep dedicated bins and bags in my house that I gradually fill with things that no longer fit or that I want to give away or consign. Most public libraries take book donations. There are bins galore in most metropolitan neighborhoods, placed by charities who will take your unwanted textiles and put them to good use. The clothing giant H&M has a campaign to give shoppers in their stores a discount when they turn in used clothing. There are plenty of good places to put your unused clothing. Goodwill, the Salvation Army, and other charities will take household goods. I recently sent to UNICEF's "Change for Good" program leftover foreign coins I had from various trips. Donating what you do not need will help you, the environment, and someone who could use the items.

Physically, I have intentionally slowed down, trying to be more acutely aware of my steps and actions. It is another aspect of simplifying my life.

The actions I have taken to simplify my life allow me to have less distraction, less to clean, and less to be responsible for in general. I now have more time to seek fulfillment in relationships, experiences, and social causes, instead of in things.

Experiences enhance our lives more than material goods do. We are, in some ways, the sum of our experiences, not the sum of what we possess.

Can you break free from the tyranny of things? Commit to donating or discarding two things for every one thing you bring into your home. Be more conscious of how you spend your time and your money. Bringing lunch to work each day can save me more than $2,000 a year.[9] How is that for a raise?

46. Good Company

> *Friendship is born at that moment when one person says to another: "What! You too? I thought I was the only one."*
>
> —C. S. Lewis

I finally learned that "No" is a complete sentence. I no longer need to justify myself to anyone. I used to make excuses and apologize when someone asked me to do something I did not want to do. Now I can just say, "No, thank you."

I also learned to surround myself with people who help me be the best version of myself that I can be. That may be intuitive to many of you. But as a people-pleasing, codependent person, this lesson took many years to sink into my psyche.

A saying often heard in the 12-step rooms is: "If you hang around in a barbershop, you eventually will get a haircut." So I avoid people, places, and things that trigger negative aspects of my personality. I do not drink, so I stay away—or leave early—from events that involve heavy drinking.

I learned who my real friends are, and what real friendship is about. I lost many friends during the dark days of my depression, some when I went to rehab, and still more when I got divorced. Those who stayed with me despite everything remain in my life today.

Learning how to say no for me was a radical act of self-care. As a people-pleaser, this was difficult for me to learn how to do. Self-care is in many ways about setting boundaries, something I have not heretofore been very effective at doing. I have a canned response now: "Thank you, but I have other commitments." Meaning sleep. Relaxation. Writing. Nurturing important relationships, including one with myself. I realized that not saying no is dishonest. It is being untrue to myself and to the other person. It erodes our confidence and our ability to be someone whose words can be trusted.

I used to overextend myself like a crazy person. It was part of my trying to deal with feeling less than others. I had 5,000 "friends," but felt close to very few. I spread myself too thinly, and it became a detriment.

It took me a long time to appreciate that there are levels of friendship—and that it was wiser to nurture the few I care about the most. My former drinking buddies are now arm's-length friends. Our activities involved a fair amount of debauchery. Now I choose to see such friends only during daylight hours. I always have my own transportation out of social situations. As a short woman, I often get hit on the face by those who tend to spit while talking after consuming several drinks. That's sometimes my cue to leave.

We can choose with whom we spend our time. Often, we unconsciously adopt traits of the people with whom we keep company. If all of my friends were vegetarians, I would likely eat less meat. If all of my friends were full of negativity, I would likely see more things in a negative light.

Though attending 12-step meetings and confiding in my sponsor keeps my self-pity largely in check, it can rear its ugly head when I compare myself with others or to an unrealistic standard. I must only evaluate myself in relation to myself—am I a better version of myself than I was yesterday? Am I making progress? Spending my time with supportive and positive people help me keep that healthy focus.

Instead of a juice cleanse, a woman I know did a negativity cleanse. For 48 hours, she avoided news, television, social media, negative people, and negative self-talk. Periodically, I would like to do the same.

I respect myself enough now to cultivate relationships with people who help bring out the best in me. I mindfully choose with whom I want to spend my allotted time on this planet. Time is more valuable than money, yet I was doing little to protect my time. I unwittingly gave it away somewhat indiscriminately. I now guard it closely and give it to those who deserve and respect it—mostly myself.

I was told that the opposite of addiction is connection. I think hard now, though, about with whom I wish to be connected and why.

I spend most of my time with sober friends. Luckily for me, more of my "normie" friends are not partying hard anymore. We all seem to put a higher value on sleep as we get older.

True friends and family are more important than just about anything else. My view of family has expanded as well. We are allowed to have families of choice and not only families of origin. Several of my friends in recovery call the people in recovery their family. The collegiality and love I have experienced from people in the recovery rooms favors such a sentiment.

Think about if Armageddon were to arrive. Who would you want by your side? Someone you could count on, right?

In the third third of my life, quality matters more than quantity. A social worker friend of mine counseled me to put up a reminder to myself to nurture the friendships with the two or three friends who were most important to me. With whom can I be my most authentic self? Who helps me to be the best version of myself that I can be? I reach out to these women regularly. They are my priority for the precious commodity of time I have left. Ask yourself: If you had 30 days left on earth, with whom would you want to spend that time? Make a note in your calendar to try to spend time with that person every month, at least. None of us has a crystal ball that informs us which day will be our last.

47. Model Behavior

I look forward to being older, when what you look like becomes less and less an issue and what you are *is the point.*

—Susan Sarandon

I used to be vainer. I coveted attention. I had an "All About Maria" party for myself when I turned 40 that featured costume changes from every decade in which I had lived, slide shows and videos about me, Maria trivia games on the tables, and Asian food and green beer (to honor my Southeast Asian and Irish heritage). A video camera was set up to capture guest tributes—to me. Guests came in outfits from the decade in which they met me. A couple of women who met me when we were pregnant wore baby bumps under their clothes. My friends from high school wore duds from the 1980s. I reveled in the attention.

I enjoyed stylish clothes and good makeup. I got facials. I liked what I saw in the mirror.

As I entered middle age, I did not like what changes were happening to my body. I looked in the mirror less, and wore less makeup. I knew many women my age who were getting Botox treatments, tummy tucks, boob jobs, and face lifts, but did not want any of that for myself, partially because of the cost and mostly because I dry heave when undergoing anything medical. I actually fainted the first time I saw my own blood.

My friend and mentor, Iris Krasnow, challenged me to allow myself to be photographed without makeup and interviewed about my aging visage. Krasnow says, "The message I like to share is don't count on your looks because they change. Discover an inner source of energy and fulfillment that has everything to do with your heart and soul and very little to do with your exterior."[10]

Our photos were featured in a *Huffington Post* piece about women embracing their natural beauty at every age. All of the women in the piece impressed me with their view of the lines on their faces as road maps of their lives. They rejected society's ageist and sexist beauty standards and accepted their increasing wrinkles. "Aging is an honor," said one. "I think the 50s are the best of all the decades so far. You really come into your own," said another. A third noted that "in Africa, women move up in prestige as they go through menopause. It is all those years that play into your value. In Asian cultures, elders are revered. I had a friend say recently that, as an elder, you don't step out and away from people, but you take on more responsibility. You are responsible for educating and teaching and helping others."[11] I admire and learn from all of these women and women like them who have chosen to age naturally and with grace.

I also learned to become comfortable with my softer middle-aged body. After spending my 30s and 40s running almost every day and completing three marathons, I "ran" the donut-fueled Krispy Kreme 5k and took up walking. I sometimes practice the Galloway Walk Run Method.[12] It is a form of interval training. In my particular practice, I alternate walking and running each minute. I completed the Philadelphia Half Marathon this way. It is easier on one's joints and bones. I can do anything for one minute at a time. So can you.

What makes a person attractive? Many times it is attitude. With age usually comes greater confidence and, I believe, a quieter, more serene beauty. Look at Helen Mirren and Meryl Streep.

Do you embrace how you look as you age? Why not? Is it because you do not like who you are at the moment, or other underlying reasons? Think about the time and money you could save on makeup if you cut it out of your budget. Reflect on these questions and strive for clarity and ease. If you surround yourself with like-minded people, you will feel more comfortable. Most importantly, if you feel good about yourself, you inevitably will be more attractive, even to yourself.

48. With the Wind in My Hair

If you surrender to the wind, you can ride it.

—Toni Morrison

Yes, buying a car can be an indulgence. Many people can get by without one. Those in the minimalist movement promote not having cars. I drove a sports utility vehicle for many years. I do not need such a big vehicle anymore.

After my divorce, I bought the only car I have ever purchased by myself. I got a tiny car that gets fantastic mileage and has a relatively low carbon footprint. I researched the best deals. In more than 30 years of driving experience, this little car has been the easiest for me to park, even in the tightest of spaces. My car's gas mileage is impressive. Its retractable roof gives me pleasure in good weather. There is something about letting the sun warm my skin and the wind bathe my body that makes me feel more alive.

Another benefit of having a convertible is that at times when I have to transport something large in my car, I can load it through the roof, and leave the roof open, if necessary. The employees at Home Depot have been thoroughly entertained when they have seen me do this. It's the little car that could.

My exhortation to simplify in a previous section may seem at odds with my buying a car. But I live far from my place of work, and there is no public transportation that could get me there. So I "bless" you to splurge every once in a while (although, of course, you do not need my blessing), if you can afford it without going into debt. You can't take it with you, after all.

Have you ridden with the top down or even all of the windows open lately? Blast your tunes and sing at the top of your lungs. Or go out and ride a bike. Run through a field. Skip. Do a cartwheel. Let the wind mess up your hair. These simple activities are so energizing. Let these sorts of activities be part of your personal arsenal of feeling truly alive.

49. Attitude of Gratitude

If you look at what you have in life, you'll always have more.
If you look at what you don't have, you'll never have enough.

—Oprah Winfrey

It is hard to be angry and grateful at the same time. I am in the process of evolving to a state in which I appreciate all of life's challenges as playing a role in teaching me a needed lesson. I am not always successful, but I strive for progress, not perfection.

How many blessings have I taken for granted for most of my life? Through happy circumstance of being born into my family of origin, in this prosperous country, I do not want for food or other necessities. During travel in third world countries, my heart is heavy when I see the poverty in which many survive. Water is a scarce commodity in many areas, as is health care. But I have seen much joy in the faces of people living in incredibly dire circumstances.

Concentration camp survivor Viktor Frankl continues to inspire me with the attitude he adopted in the face of unspeakable conditions. Dr. Frankl, a psychiatrist, says, "Between stimulus and response there is space. In that space is our power to choose our response. In our response lies our growth and our freedom."[13] This Holocaust survivor has imparted much wisdom through his experiences and writings.

I gained perspective in recovery. I learned that most of my problems were "rich people's problems" or "first world problems." Acknowledging what I am blessed with, instead of what might be lacking, is a better way to live.

I was fascinated to learn of the tradition of Hassidic Jews to make a list of 100 things for which they are grateful. This is done first thing in the morning for those who are observant of the ritual.

Compiling gratitude lists is a regular practice I have incorporated into my life. I do a list of at least ten gratitude items each day. My children usually top that list, but good health, sunny days, my dog's companionship, and beautiful trees often make it onto my lists. Sometimes I reflect on being thankful that I can see, taste, touch, hear, and smell. I know people who have lost one of more of these senses, and do not want to take having these abilities for granted.

When I am frustrated with my children's behavior, I take time out to think of what I love about them. My son has a wonderful ability to make people laugh. He is a talented singer, actor, and dancer, and brings me great joy with his performances. My daughter's wisdom and compassion sometimes take my breath away. I remember this little gem from when she was about five years old: "Mommy, if you keep yelling, we—we—we are going to become just like you!" This little truth shot defused the situation, made us all laugh, and made me more careful to not raise my voice.

When my boyfriend or girlfriends disappoint me, I reflect on what I like about them. My boyfriend, for instance, is very careful and exacting when he does repairs around the house. When I feel impatience starting to surface, I stop to consider how lucky I am that he has these helpful skills and does things correctly the first time, allowing us greater utility of whatever it is he has fixed. The lens we choose can greatly affect our attitudes. We can amplify the good or the bad, depending on what we choose to focus on each day.

My recovery sponsor gave me a gratitude bracelet with beads I can use to count my blessings throughout the day. I also am in an online women's group where we post daily gratitude lists. Other women's lists inspire me and remind me that we can choose how we respond to what we encounter in the world. I do my best to surround myself with optimistic people.

I try to help my son and daughter cultivate an attitude of gratitude. When my children are going through a rough patch, I resist the urge to give them advice unless they ask for it. Instead, I try to ask them questions. Sometimes I ask them to talk about what the worst thing that could happen may be. That usually gets them (and me) to gain perspective on a difficulty that is not a matter of life or death. I gently ask about the positives I see in each situation. It is hard to realize in the heat of the moment that every challenge or mistake can teach us something, but I know it is true. Many believe that everything happens for a reason. It took me a long while, but I accept that now.

When I focus on what is good in my life or in another person I encounter, everything goes better. It can be the difference between safely enjoying a warm, sunny day and cursing the sun's heat as oppressive or dwelling on the health risks of getting sun. Or grumbling in traffic instead of taking the time to meditatively breathe during the break provided in your day or reflect on your good fortune of being able to have a car.

Cultivating a current of gratitude underlying everything I do is a life goal of mine. Even the attempt at this has improved my life many times over. I have included a section on gratitude lists with a couple of examples near the end of this book. This one thing can change your outlook and your life, too. It costs you nothing to think of things for which you are grateful and the dividends of doing so will reverberate in your life and in the lives of those around you. You will realize that you already live an abundant life and have everything you need. As the poet Rumi says, "You wander from room to room hunting for the diamond necklace that is already around your neck."[14] I know I did.

50. Following My New Road Map

> *Two roads diverged in a wood, and I—I took the one less traveled by, and that has made all the difference.*

—Robert Frost

About once every five years for several decades, I had a similar conversation with my best friend about being uneasy with my life. Something did not feel right. I felt that much of my social engagement was superficial and that living a country club lifestyle did not fit who I am. I chipped away at that malaise in some ways, but I did not make any drastic changes in my life until I turned 50. I can see now that I engaged in self-sabotage. Out of crisis, however, can come change. I wish I had not waited for that to happen.

Perhaps the most important post-50 change I made was that I forgave myself and began living a life authentic to me. I removed the mask and discarded the persona I frequently adopted when in public, mistakenly regarding my true self as somehow inferior. I realized the need to let go of what I thought I wanted and the fantasy life I had constructed. Instead, I embrace what I have and love my life as it is, not what I wish it would be. I enjoy my life. It is the sweet spot before my body starts to fail me with old age and attendant infirmity.

I stopped trying to prove something and learned to just *be*, which sounds easy, but was not, for this multitasker extraordinaire. Before I turned 50, I seldom could enjoy a television show without simultaneously browsing a magazine, doing needlepoint, or examining my to-do list. I would be lying to say it is easy for me now to simply be in the present, although I have made much progress. I know that awareness of an issue is the first step toward changing something.

I stopped judging myself so harshly. In our society, and as humans, we are conditioned to judge. We learn survival techniques by avoiding danger, for instance. We hire people and purchase goods and services based on how we believe they will perform, given what information is available to us, including past experience. But the level of self-hatred I yoked myself with was debilitating and served no good purpose. I consciously shed it every day.

I believe, as many others do, that positivity attracts positivity. If we build good karma, we will receive it in return. Perhaps the best-known treatment of the law of attraction is in the movie and book, *The Secret*, by Rhonda Byrne.[15] Byrne posits that one's positive thoughts are powerful magnets that attract wealth, health, and happiness. I am not sure I would go that far, but I do enjoy what positive thinking is doing for my life. I try to see the good in all situations.

I started truly living the Twelve Steps. I believe the Twelve Steps are a guide for living that all should follow. Even if you are not an addict of some sort, I implore you to check out some of the Twelve Step literature, and to attend an open meeting.

The Steps involve trust in a Higher Power, working on one's character flaws, taking personal inventory, and helping others. I apply the Twelve Steps to anything in my life that is off-balance. I made amends even to people to whom I did not want to make amends, because doing whatever I can to clean up my side of the street is an important part of recovering from the disease of alcoholism or addiction in general.

The Twelve Steps are not static. I will go through the Steps with my sponsor many times over the course of my life. The first time was the hardest. I unearthed and admitted all the things I had done that had kept me mired in shame. Much to my surprise, as I listed this parade of horribles, she often nodded and said she had done the same thing. When I share something from my past in a women's meeting, like the dangerous experience of blacking out and waking up somewhere completely foreign to me, I see nods of agreement and sounds of empathetic recognition around the room. Speaking out about past sexual, emotional, and physical abuse I experienced, like the rape when I was seventeen years old by a popular football team captain, helps me heal. And now that I have witnessed so many other women's stories, I don't feel so aberrant or alone. I finally have dropped that rock of shame.

The second time I went through the Steps, I was able to see how my character flaws can morph over time or change to different ones altogether. For example, I felt pride that I was no longer drinking to oblivion, yet I judged my old drinking buddies. At least now I take time to be aware of and address these flaws. What better way to live my life than to keep trying to improve it—and me? Each year, I take a specific inventory for myself of whether and how I am being the best version of myself that I can be.

My sponsor helps keep me on track. My writing accountability partner helps me keep producing, in accordance with the goals we each have set for ourselves. We check in with each other online when we have time-sensitive benchmarks we want to reach or deadlines we have to meet. Find a person or a group who can help you stay focused on goals you set for yourself. It really helps, with just about anything. If I want to exercise regularly, committing to meeting a friend for scheduled walks or at a yoga class gets me out the door.

I write letters of thanks to the many guides I have had along the way. On each Thanksgiving, I handwrite a letter to someone I am grateful to have in my life. The art of letter writing is slowly dying in this digital age. At least once a year I do my part to keep this lovely practice alive.

I pay forward good works and deeds. I look for ways to be of service to others.

One way I give back what has been given to me is by sponsoring other women in recovery from drugs and alcohol. We speak heart to heart. I guide the women through the Twelve Steps that saved my life. Sometimes it feels as if my Higher Power is speaking through me as things come out of my mouth out of nowhere and seem to be just what my sponsee needs to hear in that moment. We share at the deepest level. We heal.

Some of my most profound service experience occurs when I help women recovering from trauma, particularly rape survivors. There are so many rape and sexual assault survivors in recovery programs, probably due in part to the prevalence of alcohol and drugs in our lives and social circles. When I was in trauma counseling, I learned that one in four women in the United States will be sexually assaulted during her lifetime. Because it happened to me and I am open now about that fact, I am serving as a counselor to rape survivors. As we bear witness to each other's pain, we can move through it and not let it define us. We not only get to survive; we can thrive.

I believe we all can make a difference in someone's life. I used to volunteer in homes for the elderly, and drove a centenarian to a pool for her weekly exercise. She usually swam only two laps when on these outings, but I certainly admired her effort. The joy you can bring with one conversation with a lonely person who has no other visitors is almost overwhelming. You can change your life, and the life of someone else, for the better with even a little effort.

What sort of road map would you like to pursue? Every single one of us can do something to improve our lives, even if it is with a simple change of attitude. Read positive books or blogs; surround yourself with positive people. One need not be a Christian to find inspiration in the peace prayer attributed to Saint Francis:

Lord, make me an instrument of your peace,
Where there is hatred, let me sow love;
where there is injury, pardon;
where there is doubt, faith;
where there is despair, hope;
where there is darkness, light;
where there is sadness, joy;

O Divine Master, grant that I may not so much seek to be consoled as to console;
to be understood as to understand;
to be loved as to love.
For it is in giving that we receive;
it is in pardoning that we are pardoned;
and it is in dying that we are born to eternal life.

This prayer spoke to me as a child, and continues to do so, perhaps even more, in this third third of my life. It is a foundation upon which I try to live my life.

Start action on your 50 after 50 list and watch your life improve. Check out my website and this book's appendix for ideas when you are stymied. Experience freedom by making the most of whatever time you have left. Enjoy!

III

LESSONS AND TOOLS FOR YOUR OWN 50 AFTER 50 LIST

No one saves us but ourselves. No one can and no one may. We ourselves must walk the path.

—Buddha

So what did I learn in this year of magical doing? I sought this year to reclaim my life for myself and to find my voice. My quest to try 50 new things after turning 50 started as a selfish means of catharsis, of finding joy and purpose in my life following a period of darkness and loss. I realized from multiple conversations that my quest was of wide interest and could be of help to many others. If I help even one reader recalibrate her life and infuse it with vitality, I will have paid forward the kindness and inspiration shared with me. I will have succeeded.

First and foremost, I gained the stark clarity that it is my life and it is up to me what I do with it in whatever time I have left. As we age, we lose loved ones. We learn that we need to take advantage of the present moment. I don't want to look back on my life and see that I settled for less than I could have done. Or that I wasted the precious commodity of time doing things I did not care about and that did not bring me closer to being the person I want to be. At the end of my life, I do not want to look back wistfully at what might have been. This year has shown me that I can still have peak experiences after five decades of life have passed.

I learned that, with an open mind and spirit, there is much abundance that can arrive in my life. When one door opens, many more doors follow. Before this transformational time in my life, I could not have imagined the people I have met and the joy of the experiences I have had. I try to approach the things I encounter with a sense of wonder and gratitude.

The beauty of growing up in this generation is the breadth of our choices. We can chapter our lives. We can make more opportunities for ourselves.

Once my basic needs were filled, I came to realize that material acquisitions do not bring lasting happiness. The wise monk and interfaith scholar, Brother David Steindl-Rast, reminds me that if I am grateful, I act out of a sense of enough and not out of a sense of scarcity. "Happiness does not make us grateful; gratitude makes us happy."[1] Each moment is a gift and an opportunity. We can avail ourselves of this opportunity or miss it. He reminds me that the key to happiness is in my own hands. Now I seek to stop and savor each experience, and not to focus on acquiring material things. I seek not to rush through life failing to "open my senses for this wonderful richness that is given to us," and to enjoy what life is giving me, moment by moment.[2]

I acknowledge that I have a certain amount of privilege to have been allowed so many choices. I am well educated. I am half Caucasian, which has given me a modicum of attendant white privilege. I am resourceful and employed. My children are grown. Had they still been dependent upon me, I would not have been willing to take as many risks as I did, or to travel as much as I did. I have lived a full life, and am no longer terrified of dying.

I am grateful for my many blessings, and I hope that I am not off-putting to you in the many things I have chosen to do after turning 50. I have two dear friends who sometimes use the hashtag, #ImNotMaria, as shorthand for my doing too much at any given time, or my ability to juggle many things at once. I have enough self-awareness now to know—and to be OK with—the fact that not everyone will like me or agree with me, or have the financial means, desire, or energy to do some of the things I suggest in this book. But my hope for you is that this book will encourage you to do whatever you can to make the most of the time you have left here.

There is so much I didn't understand in my life as it was happening. It is only in hindsight, and with life experience, that things make sense to me now. As a young person, I didn't know what I didn't know! I equated only pleasure with happiness. Now I seek a more lasting serenity. I do wish the young Maria knew what the current Maria knows.

A former nurse, Bronnie Ware, has written about the most commonly expressed five things her dying patients shared with her at the end of their lives:

1. *I wish I'd had the courage to live a life true to myself, not the life others expected of me.*
2. *I wish I hadn't worked so hard.*
3. *I wish I'd had the courage to express my feelings.*
4. *I wish I had stayed in touch with my friends.*
5. *I wish I had let myself be happier.*[3]

I am working hard to make sure these regrets are not mine when my time comes.

When my daughter was little, I started collecting advice in a journal from trusted women on what they wish they had known when they were teenagers. I gave my daughter the journal when she turned 13. If it saved her from only one mistake, I believe it did the job I intended it to do. If you are inspired to maximize the quality of the time you have left in this life after reading this book, I will have succeeded with this as well.

A friend from college suddenly died this year after a fall. He fell from a ladder while helping his mother with a home repair. He died instantly. It was the day of his 25th wedding anniversary. His eulogy was moving. I had no idea that he was a deeply spiritual and religious man. The church was packed with people who had been touched by his many kindnesses.

Do you ever wonder how you will be remembered when you die? What will your legacy be?

I try to live each day as if it were my last, though that is impracticable in some ways. But events such as my friend's recent funeral remind me that it is quality and not always quantity that matters most. I do not let opportunities go by to show and tell those I love how I feel. I try every day to make the world better because I was here. I would like to make a huge impact on the world by alleviating suffering in some way. In the meantime, I'm endeavoring to bloom where I am planted with good works and deeds, and to appreciate every day I am given on this earth.

The one that I was is no more. I learned from my past. I made peace with my skeletons and let go of my anger and regret. And I have distilled the wisdom gleaned through my 50 new things into the following top ten life lessons:

1. Be authentic to yourself. It took me a long time (unfortunately about 50 years) to figure out what that meant for me. I felt I had to prove myself to the world. I didn't feel "good enough," so I wore many masks. But we all are enough. I choose now to LOVE OUT LOUD.
2. Follow your passion in life. The happiest people I know are doing things they enjoy. The days may sometimes seem long, but the years are short. Make the most of your time on earth! We never know which day will be our last. Each day is a precious gift.
3. You are responsible for your own happiness. No one else can do it. Real happiness comes from within. I forgive myself and I love myself, as I am a child of God/the Universe. And if you can accept the things you cannot change, you will experience peace.

4. Respect yourself. Surround yourself with people who help you to become the best version of yourself. If the apocalypse arrived, who would you want by your side? Friends and family are more important than any material pursuit.

5. Much of our society runs on connections and relationships. Conduct yourself with propriety, especially in this Internet age. Never put in writing or on the web what you wouldn't mind the world seeing. If you come from a place of love and kindness, you are unlikely to do harm.

6. Practice the pause before speaking, writing, or sending. If you don't have anything to hide, life is much easier. And we are more likely to do the right thing if we examine our motivations before acting.

7. What others think of me is none of my business. You cannot know what is going on with others. Their reality is not yours. You are responsible for your actions, but not for how they are perceived by others. As we say in recovery, "to thine own self be true."

8. Practice mindfulness and meditation. Appreciate the beauty around you. Especially when you feel unsettled or upset, focus on your breath. Breathe deeply. It will center and ground you. Be present in the moment. All we really ever have is the Now.

9. Be grateful. An attitude of gratitude changes everything. I wake up every morning and think of ten things for which I am grateful, from the profound to the mundane. I can walk, I can taste, I can see—we are extraordinarily lucky.

10. Cultivate your spirituality. You can talk to your Higher Power all day long. You can find your Higher Power anywhere. Rejoice in this life God has given you, and let the light of the Spirit shine through you.

I wish I had internalized these lessons before more than half of my life was spent. But it is not over yet. None of us has to wait until our lives are in shambles before making significant changes.

My overarching goal in my post-50 life is to make this world better because I was here. I believe you can do the same.

For those of you still feeling some resistance to acting, consider this powerful verse from the late Irish poet, John O'Donohue:

For a New Beginning

In out-of-the-way places of the heart,
Where your thoughts never think to wander,

This beginning has been quietly forming,
Waiting until you were ready to emerge.
For a long time it has watched your desire,
Feeling the emptiness growing inside you,
Noticing how you willed yourself on,
Still unable to leave what you had outgrown.
It watched you play with the seduction of safety
And the gray promises that sameness whispered,
Heard the waves of turmoil rise and relent,
Wondered would you always live like this.
Then the delight, when your courage kindled,
And out you stepped onto new ground,
Your eyes young again with energy and dream,
A path of plenitude opening before you.
Though your destination is not yet clear
You can trust the promise of this opening;
Unfurl yourself into the grace of beginning
That is at one with your life's desire.
Awaken your spirit to adventure;
Hold nothing back, learn to find ease in risk;
Soon you will be home in a new rhythm,
For your soul senses the world that awaits you.[4]

Amen! Now is our time. Time is the one thing you cannot get back. Whether you are on the cusp of retirement or just getting going in your career, create a life worth living. Do not waste whatever time you have left. Do not merely settle. Find your bliss. Start now.

STARTING YOUR LIST

May your choices reflect your hope, not your fears.

—Nelson Mandela

Sometimes it takes a life-jarring event or a bad health diagnosis to get a person to make any significant changes. If you have been lucky enough not to suffer such things, do you really want to wait until something awful happens before taking steps to elevate your life? I have had several biopsies lately and it feels like a roulette wheel. Will cancer be found this time, I wonder?

Overall life expectancy has increased, but we cannot bank on numbers. At this point in our lives, we are likely to have lost dear friends or family members. Such experiences can be catalysts for change in our own lives.

It is easy to make excuses about why we cannot do something. Many of us are caring for our aging parents, for example. But that does not mean we cannot do things for ourselves. In fact, practicing self-care helps us to better care for others. On flights, we are always commanded to put on our own oxygen masks before helping others with their masks. What gives your life oxygen?

Women are generally very adept at adjusting and recalibrating. Ask yourself if your life is as you would like it to be. If not, cut out the things that no longer feed your spirit. How do you want the rest of your life to go? Do you want to ease into a gentle retirement? Or are you fulfilled by dynamicism and excitement? Or a combination of these? Pause and assess the alchemy of your life.

Let this chapter of your life be about you. Brainstorm a list of 50 things you've always wanted to try that are within the realm of possibility. If you are 60 years old, challenge yourself to do 60 new things. I would like to find a cure for cancer and achieve world peace, but those goals are outside of my skill set. Your list can include lofty goals, but can be as simple as beautifying your garden or making a small altar of things that inspire you. But please choose some badass mama things that will challenge you outside your comfort zone.

I have a friend who learned to ride a bicycle at age 57, having given up cycling when her bike was stolen 50 years prior. She crashed more than a few times, but the pride she displays when she talks about cycling and the joy it brings her are worth the bumps and bruises she sustained. For her, this was the best activity to start with on her post-50 enlivening journey.

Prioritize the items on your list. Evaluate the feasibility of each (consider time, distance, and money required). Get an accountability partner to help motivate you and keep you moving forward on your list. I started my list on my cell phone. Some people find making vision boards[5] help inspire and remind them of what they would like to manifest. Check out the appendix (for sample lists from two of my dear friends and lists of more things I want to try and things I tried before turning 50), my Fifty After 50 Facebook page, and my website, www.MariaLeonardOlsen.com for more ideas.

When you are ready to share your list, join my reader challenge. Check my website and Fifty After 50 Facebook page for details. We will cheer you on every step of the way!

Below are some areas of inquiry to get you brainstorming. Grab a notebook or a journal and start your list. Give yourself permission to change your list and let it be an organic document. You undoubtedly will be more successful with your pursuits if you believe you can do them. Even if not every item on your list goes completely as planned, you will be happier if you dared to try it. It's your life; it's up to you what you do with it!

PLACES I WANT TO GO

Look at a map of the world. If money were not a concern, where would you like to go? Why? What would you like to see or do there? Which are feasible, given time, finances, and other commitments?

You need not do them all in one year. Prioritize your list of favorites. But start dreaming now, before it is too late. Part of the thrill of travel includes the anticipation before you even step out of the door.

Do some research. I thought an African safari would be out of the question. But I have become quite adept at traveling on a shoestring budget. If you have never done that before, take a look at some of the Lonely Planet travel guides, or others like it. There are many ways to travel on a budget if you are willing to do the legwork to find out how to do so. You also could volunteer abroad with an organization. There is a wide range of volunteer vacation opportunities available, for varying lengths of time.

Regarding air travel, before you take a flight, make sure you are signed up for that airline's flight award program so you get credit for every flight you take. You can get free flights this way. Always check a site like Kayak.com to see if traveling a day earlier or later would save you money.

Once there, walk as much as possible. Not only does it save on transportation fees, but you will see more than if you simply took taxis around the area. I have happened upon such joyful surprises while on foot.

Make a list of places you want to see before you die. If you do not know where to start, check out travel websites, magazines, blogs, and books. Ask friends and acquaintances to share with you the most interesting, placid, or life-changing places to which they have traveled. Life is short! Go for it!

THINGS I HAVE WANTED TO TRY

What are some things you have wanted to try, but were worried about what other people would think? I endured some negative comments about my decision to get my motorcycle license, but riding is one of the most exhilarating experiences of my adult life. One of the gifts of aging should be letting go of other people's expectations of you. We no longer have the luxury of seemingly endless time, and do not know how long we physically will be able to do certain things that require strength or copious amounts of energy, so drop that rock that may be holding you back.

Have you wondered what the world looks like from the basket beneath a hot air balloon? Groupon and other discount coupons have made that experience more affordable. Want to learn how to train a dog? Volunteer at an institution that does dog training. This and other skills may be available as online or community college courses as well.

Take a look at your community college's or community center's course offerings. The catalog alone may give you some good ideas for your list of 50.

Learning a new skill is empowering. It keeps our brains firing and makes us more interesting, multifaceted people—even to ourselves. As we age, there will come a time when fewer things are physically possible. My mother's recent hip replacement and heart bypass operation remind me of this fact. So let us drink fully from the cup of life.

Start your list of things you have wanted to try. The list need not be final. Just imagine what you might find if you let yourself be free to try, especially if you were not burdened by other people's opinion of what you choose. Remember, what other people think of us is not our responsibility.

GOALS

"Life is what happens to you while you're busy making other plans," said John Lennon. Life circumstances prevent many of us from completing earlier goals. Life also requires us sometimes to adjust our plans.

Our generation is lucky to be able to chapter our lives in a way that was not easy to do for our mothers. Many women today step off the career track while raising children then can reenter the workforce in the same or a different capacity. I cannot say I love practicing law. But I enjoy using my skills to help people resolve their problems and the lawyer's salary that affords me opportunities I would not otherwise have.

I certainly never planned to get divorced. In fact, it was a life goal of mine never to divorce. Thus, I had to reformulate my view of my "happily ever after." Thankfully, with much work, I was able to find happiness within myself. Figuring out what truly makes you happy will inform your goals. Meditate on that, then start writing.

What are some goals you have wanted to fulfill, but haven't achieved—yet?

MORE!

My lists and journal prompts are not meant to be exhaustive. One of the greatest gifts of feminism is the ability women have to choose. We are less shackled by limiting norms of generations prior. We do not have to move noiselessly into irrelevance or retirement. So, brainstorm about other things you would like to try in your post-50 years. Let the list be reflective of your evolution, as you open your mind to the possibilities and start doing mind-expanding, enlivening things.

Consider jotting down other things you are thinking about doing (but may need time and/or money before you can do them). Reflect on anything you do not love about your current life situation. What can you change about such things? What are some ways of effecting these changes?

The Dalai Lama, when asked what surprised him most about humanity, answered,

> Man. Because he sacrifices his health in order to make money. Then he sacrifices money to recuperate his health. And then he is so anxious about the future that he does not enjoy the present; the result being that he does not live in the present or the future; he lives as if he is never going to die, and then dies having never really lived.

GRATITUDE LISTS

Make a daily list of things for which you are grateful, from the prosaic (the sun is out today; I can still see/hear/taste/read) to the profound (my best friend, the love of my partner). If you wake up every day and think of a few things for which you are grateful, it will set a better tone for the rest of your day. We all know people who seem to have everything, but they are not happy, as well as people who have experienced great loss or have little, but are deeply happy. Why? Because they are grateful for what they have in their lives. They are grateful to be alive.[6] I ask my sponsees in early recovery to text me every day with at least one thing for which they are grateful. You, too, can have a gratitude buddy, or start your own gratitude journal. It will make everything you do in this new life even better when you take the time to relish and appreciate it. Cultivating an attitude of gratitude every day can rewire your brain into a more positive mode. You can focus on the things that are good in your life instead of spending time wanting more. Your life is happening right now. Make this the first day of your amazing new chapter. . . .

Suggested Reading

*P*ost-50, these books helped me more than any others. They continue to inspire me.

Man's Search for Meaning, by Viktor Frankl (Boston: Beacon, 2006).
    Dr. Frankl's book was introduced to me in rehab and changed my life. A Holocaust survivor, Dr. Frankl maintains that we cannot avoid suffering, but we can choose how we cope with it, find meaning in it, and move forward with renewed purpose. Favorite quote: "Everything can be taken from a man but one thing: the last of the human freedoms—to choose one's attitude in any given set of circumstances, to choose one's own way."

The Four Agreements: A Practical Guide to Personal Freedom (A Toltec Wisdom Book), by don Miguel Ruiz (San Rafael, CA: Amber-Allen, 1997).
    Four ways to improve your life exponentially. By adopting these four practices, we release our suffering and prevent pain.

The Way to Love: The Last Meditations of Anthony de Mello, by Anthony de Mello (New York: Image Books, Doubleday, 1995).
    Powerful meditations on the meaning of true love. I benefited greatly from the explanation of nonattachment as being critical to one's happiness. I have given this book out to several friends who have found themselves in unhealthy relationships.

Learned Optimism: How to Change Your Mind and Your Life, by Martin E. P. Seligman (New York: Vintage, 2006).

I was introduced to Seligman's positive psychology and theory of learned helplessness when I was fighting depression. This book was, and remains, a tremendous life tool for me.

Spirit Junkie: A Radical Road to Self-Love and Miracles, by Gabrielle Bernstein (New York: Harmony, 2012).

Bernstein presents the classic work, *A Course in Miracles*, to the next generation of seekers, while describing her own transformational journey. She preaches the miracle of forgiveness, and helped me let go of the stronghold of ego. Favorite quote: "If one chooses to see the darkness in others, we amplify the darkness in ourselves."

Alcoholics Anonymous (New York: Works Publishing, 1939).

Colloquially known as the "Big Book," it is the official explanation of the program of Alcoholics Anonymous and stories of recovering alcoholics. It is truly inspired writing that has saved many an addict from relapsing into the fatal disease, and is something I refer to often. It is now in its fourth edition.

Co-Dependent No More: How to Stop Controlling Others and Start Caring for Yourself, by Melody Beattie (Center City, MN: Hazelden, 1987).

How to free yourself from codependence on other people, via self-care, boundary setting, and detachment with love.

The Language of Letting Go: Daily Meditations for Codependents, by Melody Beattie (Center City, MN: Hazelden, 1990).

Daily inspirational readings on the importance of emotional and spiritual self-care. Reminders that help me every day. There is a multitude of daily reading books, but this one has helped me the most.

Bibliography

Alcoholics Anonymous. *Alcoholics Anonymous*. New York: Works Publishing, 1939.

Alcoholics Anonymous World Services. *Daily Reflections*. New York: Alcoholics Anonymous World Services, 1990.

———. *Twelve Steps and Twelve Traditions*. New York: Alcoholics Anonymous World Services, 1981.

B., Mel. *Walk in Dry Places*. Center City, MN: Hazelden, 1996.

Beattie, Melody. *Co-Dependent No More: How to Stop Controlling Others and Start Caring for Yourself*. Center City, MN: Hazelden, 1987.

———. *The Language of Letting Go: Daily Meditations for Codependents*. Center City, MN: Hazelden, 1990.

Bernstein, Gabrielle. *Spirit Junkie: A Radical Road to Self-Love and Miracles*. New York: Harmony, 2012.

Buettner, Dan. *Thrive: Finding Happiness the Blue Zones Way*. Washington, DC: National Geographic, 2010.

Byrne, Rhonda. *The Secret*. New York: Atria Books/Beyond Words, 2006.

Cutrone, Kelly. *Normal Gets You Nowhere*. New York: HarperOne, 2012.

Dondrub, Lhamo (His Holiness the Dalai Lama). *The Art of Happiness: A Handbook for Living*. New York: Riverhead, 2009.

Estes, Clarissa Pinkola. *Women Who Run with the Wolves: Myths and Stories of the Wild Woman Archetype*. New York: Ballantine, 1992.

Fieri, Guy. *Diners, Drive-ins, Dives: An All American Road Trip . . . With Recipes*. New York: HarperCollins, 2008.

Fonda, Jane. *My Life So Far*. New York: Random House, 2006.

France, Gary. *France in America—A 21,000 Mile USA Discovery on My Harley-Davidson*. Shrove, Greencastle, Ireland: Inis Communications, 2013.

Frankl, Viktor. *Man's Search for Meaning*. Boston: Beacon, 2006.

Gilbert, Elizabeth. *Eat, Pray, Love: One Woman's Search for Everything Across Italy, India and Indonesia*. New York: Riverhead, 2007.

Gladwell, Malcolm. *Outliers: The Story of Success*. New York: Little, Brown and Company, 2008.

Hanh, Thich Nhat. *Peace Is Every Step: The Path of Mindfulness in Everyday Life*. New York: Bantam, 1992.

Iyengar, B. K. S. *Light on Life: The Yoga Journey to Wholeness, Inner Peace, and Ultimate Freedom*. London: Rodale, 2005.

Kerouac, Jack. *On the Road*. New York: Viking Compass, 1957.

Kantrowitz, Barbara, and Pat Wingert. *The Menopause Book*. New York: Workman, 2009.

Krasno, Jeff. *Wanderlust—A Modern Yogi's Guide to Discovering Your Best Self*. New York: Rodale, 2015.

Krasnow, Iris. *Surrendering to Yourself: You Are Your Own Soulmate*. New York: Miramax, 2003.

Lamott, Anne. *Help, Thanks, Wow: The Three Essential Prayers*. New York: Penguin, 2012.

Markham, Beryl. *West with the Night: A Memoir*. New York: North Point, 2013.

de Mello, Anthony. *The Way to Love: The Last Meditations of Anthony de Mello*. New York: Image Books, Doubleday, 1995.

Melton, Glennon Doyle. *Love Warrior*. London: Two Roads, 2016.

O'Donohue, John. *To Bless the Space Between Us: A Book of Blessings*. New York: Doubleday, 2008.

Patchett, Ann. *This Is the Story of a Happy Marriage*. New York: HarperCollins, 2013.

Pirsig, Robert M. *Zen and the Art of Motorcycle Maintenance: An Inquiry into Values*. New York: Bantam, 1976.

Rubin, Gretchen. *The Happiness Project: Or, Why I Spent a Year Trying to Sing in the Morning, Clean My Closets, Fight Right, Read Aristotle, and Generally Have More Fun*. New York: Harper, 2011.

Ruiz, don Miguel. *The Four Agreements: A Practical Guide to Personal Freedom (A Toltec Wisdom Book)*. San Rafael, CA: Amber-Allen, 1997.

———. *The Four Agreements Companion Book: Using the Four Agreements to Master the Dream of Your Life (Toltec Wisdom)*. San Rafael, CA: Amber-Allen, 2000.

Seligman, Martin E. P. *Learned Optimism: How to Change Your Mind and Your Life*. New York: Vintage, 2006.

Sincero, Jen. *You Are a Badass: How to Stop Doubting Your Greatness and Living an Awesome Life*. Philadelphia, PA: Running Press, 2013.

Steves, Rick. *Asia Through the Back Door*. Santa Fe, NM: John Muir, 1993.

Strayed, Cheryl. *Wild: From Lost to Found on the Pacific Crest Trail*. New York: Vintage, 2013.

Theroux, Paul. *The Great Railway Bazaar*. New York: Ballantine, 1975.

Tolle, Eckhart. *The Power of Now: A Guide to Spiritual Enlightenment*. Vancouver, BC: Namaste, 1999.

Weiner, Eric. *The Geography of Bliss: One Grump's Search for the Happiest Places in the World*. New York: Twelve, 2009.

White, E. B. *Here Is New York*. New York: The Little Bookroom, 1999.

Appendix

Additional Sample Lists from Others Inspired by My List of 50

I have worked with a number of women to help them enhance this chapter of their lives. Together, we have brainstormed custom lists and have cheered each other on as we try each new thing. Here are two of my favorites, a list of more things I want to try, and more suggestions for you of enjoyable things I tried before turning 50.

Hilary Olsen's List of 50 After 50

1. Cooking lessons in Italy
2. Learned to let go of worries about money
3. Had individual talks with my adult children to ensure no misunderstandings or resentments remain
4. Facilitated more communication among family members
5. Learned how to design and make floor cloths
6. Took a trip with my ex-sister-in-law to Costa Rica
7. Took up yoga
8. Worked on nurturing friendships with other empty-nesters
9. Joined a movie-going club
10. Made a more concerted effort to say yes instead of no
11. Sewed 18 pink "pussy hats" to support the National Women's March
12. Became an ESL tutor
13. Visited ex-sister-in-law at her house near the bay
14. Let go of resentments toward family members
15. Took more advantage of things
16. Allowed my friend to convince me to do an eyebrow makeover (and then returned to my regular brows)

17. Adopted more kittens
18. Edited a book
19. Took piano lessons
20. Used city bikes to get around Boston and other cities
21. Started rewarding myself with professional therapeutic massages
22. Joined a gym
23. Wore more fashionable low-rise undies with my low-rise jeans
24. Traveled alone to the U.K.
25. Started writing newsletters about my cancer treatment to keep my loved ones up to date
26. Joined a support group for women with cancer
27. Did a zip line over the treetops, despite my fear
28. Tried pot brownies (and promptly fell asleep)
29. Wore my pajamas to take someone to the train station without caring about the reactions of others
30. Celebrated my 50th birthday in the Caribbean with my three best friends
31. Sold clothing on consignment websites
32. Learned how to ask for help
33. Came to terms with my body as it is, rather than wishing it were thinner
34. Finishing my degree for myself, not for other people
35. Visited Machu Picchu
36. Learned to say what I want
37. Gave myself permission to nap when tired
38. Learned to accept compliments
39. Learned to believe such compliments were true
40. Let go of some of the worry about my children
41. Took more long, luxurious bubble baths
42. Hitchhiked!
43. Did a woo-woo spiritual dance class that was outside my comfort zone
44. Experimented with new recipes
45. Took a tiny prop plane to an island
46. Did some kayaking
47. Enjoyed the simple pleasure of gardening
48. Paid more attention to being grateful, especially for the wonderful doctors and nurses at Dana Farber
49. Allowed myself to be adopted by a church group, even though I don't believe in religion

50. Learned to stay hopeful even when cancer lives in my body, and to make the most of each day that I have here

Sandy Thackston's List of 60 After 60

1. Learned how to be comfortable in solitude
2. Caught myself in denial about certain things in my life and let myself see things clearly
3. Learned to practice self-care
4. Learned to address my codependence
5. Did a sugar cleanse
6. Took up painting again
7. Got some painful but necessary dental work done that I had dreaded and put off for a long time
8. Got myself back into the gym
9. Got honest about painful things in my life
10. Started working on my own problems instead of deflecting by focusing on other people's problems
11. Allowed myself to be pampered at a spa
12. Started to get rid of stuff in my house that I no longer need
13. Marched in the National Women's March
14. Campaigned for a presidential candidate I believe in
15. Campaigned in another state for a presidential candidate
16. Joined a women's group to do what I can to combat the inequality and bigotry the current president espouses
17. Sold things on Craigslist
18. Coauthored an article about "Bethesda rednecks"
19. Started a salon for the exchange of ideas
20. Allowed other women to bear witness to my pain
21. Gave up smoking
22. Gave up vaping
23. Wore "wing" eyeliner even though my daughter poked fun at me for doing so
24. Successfully lost weight
25. Visited the new National Museum for African American History and Culture
26. Helped many women who are trying to get sober
27. Helped my daughter learn how to do real estate closings
28. House trained my dog
29. Detached from people who are not serious about their sobriety

30. Evaluated what I want my life to look like in five years and made changes necessary to make it that way
31. Reclaimed my attic office that had become overstuffed with storage items
32. Learned about LGBT issues by listening to my friends' LGBT radio program
33. Started gardening
34. Became a confirmation sponsor
35. Learned how to stay alone and not be afraid
36. Finally realized that I deserve more
37. Dealt with my sugar addiction
38. Gave up soda
39. Curtailed my buying habits
40. Read more books
41. Became more politically active and aware
42. Separated myself from toxic people
43. Started cooking meals just for myself
44. Gave up social media for Lent
45. Had a yard sale and gave away a lot of things I no longer need
46. Took a reflection retreat for a week by myself to my friend's house near the water
47. Celebrated my 60th birthday in grand style with my daughters, a fancy hotel suite, and a limo
48. Donated to charity a lot of things I have not used in years
49. Practiced tough love on a relative who violated our house rules
50. Had a long-overdue discussion with a family member about unacceptable behavior
51. Dwelled on gratitude for small blessings, like my high-pressure shower head that is so much better than the water-saving one my father made us use when I was growing up
52. Got better at accepting compliments without protesting
53. Took up walking for exercise
54. Learned how to unplug after a certain time each night
55. Worked on saying no more often
56. Spoke my truth
57. Asked for help when I needed it
58. Worked with women dedicated to their recovery
59. Shed relationships with women who were not dedicated to their recovery
60. Researched other possibilities for my career path

MORE THINGS I WOULD LIKE TO EXPERIENCE IN THE YEARS AHEAD

1. Give a TedTalk
2. Take a lifesaving course
3. Go to an ashram
4. Go on a silent retreat
5. Learn how to do a handstand (not strong enough to do so, yet!)
6. See the Northern Lights
7. Go to Angkor Wat in Cambodia
8. Take a cooking course in Italy with my best friend
9. Rent a house in Tuscany
10. Live abroad
11. Take a boat safety course
12. Visit Mauritius, the Canary Islands, Portugal, Prague, Istanbul, Tibet, Belize, the Grenadines, Banff, the Maldives, Egypt, Bora Bora, Anguilla, Barcelona, Antarctica, Virgin Gorda, the Seychelles, Mallorca and Petra, Jordan
13. Attend an Asian lantern festival and release a lantern into the sky
14. See a moose in the wild (believe me, I have tried!)
15. Experience the community at a Burning Man festival in the California desert
16. Paint a huge canvas, bigger than myself
17. Be a guest on the *Today Show*
18. Go to a Rolling Stones concert
19. Tour the United States in a recreational vehicle
20. Listen more often than talk
21. Get my scuba certification
22. Hear the Dalai Lama speak
23. Try an Omega retreat and one at Kripalu and Shambhala Mountain Center
24. Retire somewhere warm
25. Become proficient at another language
26. Revisit the children's library I helped to build in the poorest region of Nepal
27. Beat my sugar addiction
28. Tap maple syrup from a tree
29. Stare up at the tall trees of the Redwood forest
30. Make a soufflé
31. Go sand skiing

32. Visit the 14 states I have not yet spent any time in
33. Host grandparent camp for my grandchildren (if I am lucky enough to have grandchildren!)
34. Drive a snowmobile
35. Try snowboarding
36. Learn how to paint believable-looking clouds and water
37. Visit the largest living tortoises in the Galapagos Islands (Ecuador)
38. Spend some time in the town reputed to be the happiest place in America: San Luis Obispo, California (according to author and *National Geographic* lecturer Dan Buettner)
39. Learn calligraphy
40. Ride on a camel
41. Watch the wild pony migration in Assateague, Maryland
42. Successfully propagate succulent plants
43. Ride on Pacific Coast Highway 1 between Los Angeles and San Francisco on a motorcycle
44. Stay in a yurt in Big Sur
45. Create something beautiful out of glass mosaic
46. See Niagara Falls from the Canadian side
47. Write a 60 After 60 book, and continue the series for other decades
48. Watch my former foster son graduate from college and do what I can to help him get there
49. Complete a long-term volunteer project (possibly the Peace Corps)
50. Grow my own vegetables
51. Be more intentional about anything I purchase. Consider whether it is a want or a need.
52. Learn how to eat slowly and put my fork down between every bite, savoring the flavors
53. Participate in the Holi Festival of Colors (a Hindu color festival involving the throwing of colored powder in a joyful celebration and/ or color run)
54. Learn how to belly dance
55. Learn how to play a guitar
56. Find lost relatives
57. Experience zero gravity
58. Participate in a flash mob dance
59. Have no regrets
60. Stay open to more possibilities and viewpoints
61. Practice self-care
62. Try hang-gliding
63. Float in the Dead Sea

64. Successfully be able to do the crow and other challenging positions in yoga
65. Learn more about Judaism and incorporate Shabbat practice into my life
66. Go sky diving from an airplane
67. Meander through the dramatic slot canyons of Antelope Canyon on Navajo land in Arizona
68. Bake fresh bread from scratch
69. Try riding on a luge sled
70. Ride an ATV
71. Let my children learn from their mistakes instead of trying to continually make things easier for them
72. Become more immersed in Buddhist principles
73. Check my ego and intentions more often
74. Find more ways to be of service to others
75. Let more days unfold without a plan
76. Be more present

OTHER THINGS I HAVE DONE BEFORE TURNING 50 THAT I HIGHLY RECOMMEND IF YOU HAVEN'T TRIED THESE ALREADY

1. Have a dialogue with someone very different from yourself (for example, from another culture, political persuasion, nonconforming gender) and listen with an open mind to their point of view. See if you can find common ground.
2. Mentor and/or foster someone
3. Scuba (even a resort/discovery dive)
4. Bike in Provence or in the California wine country
5. Visit the Taj Mahal at dawn, before the crowds arrive
6. Go whitewater rafting
7. Go inner tubing down a lazy river
8. View the Alaskan glaciers
9. Try stand-up paddle-boarding
10. Schedule in play time; do something completely frivolous
11. Give away things you have not used in the last year
12. Go to a planetarium or gaze through a powerful telescope at the stars and planets
13. Try surfing

14. Build a life-sized sand sculpture
15. Experience the energy of a Bruce Springsteen concert (or of any musician whose music you love). I recommend Bruce Springsteen because I have never seen an artist push himself or herself so long in concert.
16. Watch movies outdoors
17. Go parasailing
18. Jump on a trampoline
19. Visit caverns (like Luray Caverns) and marvel at the stalactites and stalagmites
20. Spend time with puppies and kittens
21. Feel the resonant organ music in one of the world's great cathedrals
22. Go kayaking
23. Pay it forward in some way, anonymously
24. Roast marshmallows or some other food on an open fire
25. Try fly-fishing
26. Hold a baby. Breathe in deeply when you do. There is nothing like the smell of a baby.
27. Treat yourself to a massage, especially a foot massage
28. Try a new type of art
29. Watch a child see a sparkler for the first time
30. Marvel at Michelangelo's artwork on the ceiling of the Sistine Chapel at the Vatican
31. Sleep under the stars
32. Enjoy sunset on a beach (as many as you can!)
33. Play with baby animals
34. Forgive
35. Fall asleep or just rest in a hammock
36. Go cross-country skiing
37. Go snowshoeing
38. Stand up for someone who lacks the courage or ability to do so
39. Serve in a soup kitchen or another charitable endeavor
40. Read to those who cannot do so
41. Try downhill skiing
42. Go water skiing
43. Fly across the water on a jet ski
44. Ride in a horse-drawn carriage
45. Do some hula hooping
46. Try the flying trapeze
47. Watch the wildebeest migration across Ngorongoro crater
48. Meet some tribal people, like the Masai
49. Swim under a waterfall
50. Learn a new dance, like the tango, jitterbug, salsa, or samba. Go ballroom dancing.

51. Learn how to play an instrument
52. Marvel at the enormity of the Grand Canyon
53. See a Broadway show
54. Reread a classic piece of literature (I love how it seems different as I age. I laughed out loud as an adult when I reread *The Catcher in the Rye.*)
55. Take in the spirituality of a Buddhist temple
56. Experience life in another country or culture that differs from yours
57. Lend your company to someone who is sick and/or lonely
58. Get outside of your comfort zone
59. Ride in a hot air balloon
60. Go snorkeling
61. Watch a glass-blower practice his craft
62. Ride an elephant
63. Walk the Highline elevated park in Manhattan
64. Travel to an underserved or poverty-stricken area. See what you can do to help.
65. Visit a nursing home and listen to some of the residents
66. Allow yourself to have an appointment with a therapist. Talk about something you have never shared before with anyone.
67. Visit the Louvre Museum in Paris and any other great museums of the world
68. Sail
69. Clean out your abode and give things away, recycle or discard them so that when you die, no one else has to do it
70. Go ice skating, roller blading, or roller skating
71. Lie in the grass, listen to the sounds around you and look at the clouds
72. Watch a living creature hatch from an egg
73. Attend an opera, symphony, and at least one ballet performance
74. Visit our country's National Parks
75. Try glamping
76. Eat something fresh from a garden
77. Go canoeing
78. Let a day unfold with no plans whatsoever
79. Make something with your hands
80. Go to Jazzfest in New Orleans (less crazy than Mardi Gras, with great music and food)
81. Swim with dolphins
82. Hand write an old-fashioned thank-you letter to someone you appreciate, like a former teacher, a good friend, or a family member
83. Watch hummingbirds, butterflies, and woodpeckers do their thing
84. Disconnect from all electronics for a period of time

85. Relax in a natural hot spring
86. Pick up trash whenever you take a walk. Think of it as a random act of kindness toward others and Mother Earth
87. Plant a garden
88. Try geocaching
89. Go on a retreat, whether organized by others or just to be away from your routine
90. Listen to someone much older than yourself describe what his or her life used to be like and the changes he or she has seen in his or her lifetime
91. Take a ride in a helicopter and/or a propeller plane
92. Sleep on a boat and let gentle waves rock you to sleep
93. Hike up a mountain or hill, or through a forest
94. Try a ropes course and/or ziplining
95. Quit taking it personally ("Q.T.I.P.")
96. Go to comedy shows, especially improv
97. Ride on a moped, scooter, or minibike
98. Walk or run a 5k, 10k, or marathon
99. Go mountain biking
100. Adopt or foster an animal that needs a home (if there is a kitten café anywhere near you, it is fun to watch the cats while you eat or drink to see which feline may be a good fit for you), and bring that animal, if possible, to visit animal lovers who cannot keep pets where they are living
101. Make peace with your childhood, lest it continue to affect your present life, even unconsciously
102. Check out a curated storytelling event (like The Moth or Story-league)
103. Make a vision board of what you want your life to look like
104. Draft a mission statement for your life. Reevaluate your current circumstances and decide whether you would like to change anything.
105. Visit someone confined to a hospital or prison and reflect on your health and freedom
106. Stand up for something you believe in, whether it is by protesting, writing, calling, or confronting
107. Reflect on the most painful or difficult thing that ever happened in your life and what that experience taught you
108. Let go!

Share your ideas on my website, www.MariaLeonardOlsen.com, or Fifty After 50 Facebook page.

Book Club Discussion Questions

$\mathscr{T}$am available to come to your book club in person or via Skype. Please contact me via the publisher, my website, www.MariaLeonardOlsen.com, or my Fifty After 50 Facebook page.

1. What do you think of Maria's list of 50 and how would it compare were you to make your own list? What have you been inspired to do?
2. Can you relate to any of the feelings Maria describes in feeling "other than" and self-consciously different from her peers? How so?
3. Can you recall some childhood cruelties inflicted upon you? Why do you think many of us sometimes remember slights from childhood more than those that occur when we are adults?
4. Do you have a bucket list? What do you think of the idea of having one?
5. What is the most challenging thing you have ever done? What did you learn from it?
6. What is holding you back from trying new things?
7. What is your definition of happiness? What are three things that make you happy?
8. Where are the top three places in the world you want to see before you die?
9. If you died today, what regrets would you have?
10. Who could be your accountability partner to spur you on to doing things on your list of 50 things?
11. How has your view of aging evolved now that you are in your fifth decade on the planet?
12. Legacies can take many forms. Artistic, philanthropic, financial, creative, and written are some. What is a legacy you would like to leave?

Acknowledgments

$\mathcal{I}$ would like to thank my sister-in-law, Hilary Olsen (technically, my ex-sister-in-law, but I will never X her from my heart), for reading an early draft and helping me navigate the self-revelatory aspects of what I was considering publishing. Thank you to dear friend Anne Christman, whose wise counsel is always of immense value. Thanks also to my best friend from childhood, Lisa Hodgkins, who gave me confidence that my book would be interesting to others. All three provided excellent edits.

Grateful acknowledgment also is given to the following: Trisha de Borchgrave, for our transatlantic interview, a continuation of her sharing her brilliant intellect, creativity, and passion for many things, including healthful eating; Iris Krasnow, for serving as my writing mentor and encouraging transformations in the best possible ways; Pleasance Silicki, for radiating joy and sharing more with me during an interview for this book about how she does it; Pat Wingert, for allowing me to interview her during a busy week that crossed over into her vacation, and for sharing her insights about the positive aspects of menopause and good advice for meeting the challenges it can bring into our lives at this juncture; and Diane Nine, my talented agent, without whom this book would not have been possible.

Thank you to my beloved children, Caroline and Christopher. I am honored to be your mother.

PERMISSIONS

E. B. White: Author of the excerpted essay, "Here Is New York." Copyright © 1949 by E. B. White. Reprinted by permission of ICM Partners.

165

Notes

PREFACE

1. don Miguel Ruiz, http://www.miguelruiz.com.

2. don Miguel Ruiz, *The Four Agreements: A Practical Guide to Personal Freedom (A Toltec Wisdom Book)* (San Rafael, CA: Amber-Allen, 1997).

3. The 12-step group of which I am a member has a tradition of anonymity that does not permit me to name it in media. The tradition, however, "does not preclude you from speaking about your own recovery." *Advocacy with Anonymity* (by Faces and Voices of Recovery, a brochure I picked up in the literature stand at a 12-step meeting), "Start by telling your story. Talk about recovery and how you achieved it. . . . People rarely see the faces of recovering alcoholics and addicts. They need to see firsthand that treatment really does work." See also https://www.ncadd.org/get-involved/advocacy/advocacy-with-anonymity, accessed August 31, 2017. I must stress, however, that I speak only for myself and not for any organization.

4. Vision Quest Writing Retreats, www.visionquestretreats.com.

PART I

1. The earliest verified variation of this quote about writing is by Paul Gallico in his 1946 book, *Confessions of a Story Writer* (New York: Alfred A. Knopf). In 1973, the quote was attributed to Ernest Hemingway in *The Craft of Writing*, by William Knott (Reston, VA: Reston Publishing). It has appeared numerous times on popular quotation websites as a quotation by Hemingway.

CHAPTER 1

1. Anti-miscegenation laws existed in 16 states until declared unconstitutional by the U.S. Supreme Court in 1967. *Loving v. Virginia*, 388 U.S. 1 (1967). My Filipina mother was considered of a different race from my Caucasian father.

2. National Sexual Violence Resource Center, http://www.nsvrc.org/sites/default/files/publications_nsvrc_factsheet_media-packet_statistics-about-sexual-violence_0.pdf.

3. See W. E. B. Du Bois, *The Souls of Black Folk* (New York: Bantam Classic, 1903).

4. don Miguel Ruiz, *The Four Agreements: A Practical Guide to Personal Freedom (A Toltec Wisdom Book)* (San Rafael, CA: Amber-Allen, 1997).

CHAPTER 2

1. *Mommy, Why's Your Skin So Brown?* (Milwaukee: Mirror, 2013); *Not the Cleaver Family—The New Normal in Modern American Families* (Mustang, OK: Tate, 2016). An article I wrote, "Being a Parent Is Not Always Apparent," was published in a local Maryland paper, and several preschools in my area gave copies of it to their parents as part of their welcoming packages.

2. Whether Roosevelt said this is debatable, but it is widely attributed to the former president. See, for example, Kenneth B. Cooper, *Becoming a Great School* (Lanham, MD: Rowman & Littlefield, 2014), ix.

3. ADAA was founded in 1979 as an international nonprofit organization dedicated to the prevention, treatment, and cure of anxiety, depressive, obsessive-compulsive, and trauma-related disorders through education, practice, and research; see www.adaa.org.

4. The National Suicide Prevention Lifeline, for example, provides free and confidential emotional support around the clock to people in suicidal crisis or emotional distress. Their toll-free number is 1-800-273-8255.

5. National Public Radio, http://www.npr.org/sections/health-shots/2011/10/20/141544135/look-around-1-in-10-americans-take-antidepressants.

6. Harvard Health Publishing, http://www.health.harvard.edu/blog/astounding-increase-in-antidepressant-use-by-americans-201110203624.

7. Drug-gene testing, also called pharmacogenomics, is starting to gain traction in the United States. Cytochrome P450 tests are beginning to be used to help patients determine how their body processes a drug, which, in turn, provides clues as to which medications may have more efficacy with a given patient. See http://www.mayoclinic.org/tests-procedures/cyp450-test/basics/definition/PRC-20013543, accessed August 31, 2017.

CHAPTER 3

1. Maria Leonard Olsen, "A Suburban Mom's Ascent from Hell," *Washingtonian*, January 22, 2013, https://www.washingtonian.com/2013/01/22/a-suburban-moms

-ascent-from-hell/. My hope in writing about my recovery is that it can help other people find help. According to the National Council on Alcoholism and Drug Dependence, "To make recovery a reality for even more Americans, we must become visible. . . . Almost two-thirds of Americans have friends or family members who have struggled with addiction to alcohol and other drugs. Together, we can break down the wall of shame and stigma that keeps people from finding their path to long-term recovery," https://www.ncadd.org/get-involved/advocacy/advocacy-with-anonymity, accessed August 31, 2017.

2. A host of fellowships to help people with various addictions uses the Twelve Steps. In other fellowships, the wording of the steps varies slightly. Although I usually do not feel the compulsion to drink, the Steps help me curb "dry drunk" behavior as well. People in recovery often use the term dry drunk to refer to restless, irritable, and discontented behavior that continues after one has stopped drinking. If we do not continue to work on our character flaws and underlying issues, many of us regress or relapse.

3. *Alcoholics Anonymous* (New York: Works Publishing, 1939, 71–72.

4. Alcoholics Anonymous, "Preamble," http://www.aa.org/assets/en_US/aa-literature/smf-92-aa-preamble.

5. *Alcoholics Anonymous.* The first time I read this book, I was taken aback by some of the anachronistic word choices and assumptions that the husband was the alcoholic and the wife the suffering spouse. Though there has been much debate on this topic, the original text has not changed significantly since the first edition. In any event, the "Big Book" contains inspired writing that has saved many an addict from the fatal disease.

6. "God, grant me the serenity to accept the things I cannot change, the courage to change the things I can, and the wisdom to know the difference." The original author of this prayer is unknown.

7. His Holiness the Dalai Lama, *The Art of Happiness: A Handbook for Living* (New York: Riverhead, 2009).

8. Matthew 6:27.

9. Jalal al-Din Rumi; see https://www.poets.org/poetsorg/poet/jalal-al-din-rumi.

10. Jalal al-Din Rumi.

11. *Alcoholics Anonymous*, 96.

CHAPTER 4

1. Codependency is an "emotional and behavioral condition that affects an individual's ability to have a healthy, mutually satisfying relationship. It is also known as 'relationship addiction' because people with codependency often form or maintain relationships that are one-sided, emotionally destructive and/or abusive." Mental Health America, www.MentalHealthAmerica.net.

2. Viktor Frankl, *Man's Search for Meaning* (Boston: Beacon, 2006).

3. There are 12-step meetings all over the world. Alcoholics Anonymous is the best known of such groups, though there are others. See http://www.aa.org. In the

Washington, D.C., metropolitan area alone, there are more than 1,600 meetings per week. See https://aa-dc.org/meetings. Online schedules, as well as online meetings, are available every day, around the clock. See http://aa-intergroup.org. It is recommended that new people try several different meetings to find one that feels like the right fit. I recently have started to become acquainted with a Buddhist-based recovery program called Refuge Recovery. See www.RefugeRecovery.com.

4. Anne Tyler, *Ladder of Years* (New York: Random House, 1995).

CHAPTER 5

1. I personally recommend the Lonely Planet book series and website for budget travel. See www.lonelyplanet.com. The Facebook group Girls LOVE Travel and Girls LOVE Travel 35+ are excellent resources as well. Airbnb has made travel more affordable, as have apps such as HotelTonight. If you have never used Airbnb, I can send you a coupon for $40 off your first trip! Contact me via www.MariaLeonardOlsen.com or on my Fifty After 50 Facebook page.

2. See, for example, http://wwoof.net/volunteer-with-wwoof-gain-skills-meet-people-travel-the-world, accessed June 22, 2017.

3. Desiree Garcia is the owner of Mobile Massage Therapy. She specializes in sports injuries and pain management, deep tissue and trigger point massage, acupressure, reflexology, and energy healing. She also is a Reiki master and yoga teacher.

4. See www.cnn.com/shows/united-shades-of-america.

5. See https://www.nytimes.com/2017/05/02/travel/how-to-make-the-most-of-a-staycation.html and https://www.realsimple.com/work-life/life-strategies/staycation#bring-spa-to-you, accessed August 30, 2017.

6. TripAdvisor also publishes regional and city travel guides. See www.TripAdvisor.com, accessed August 25, 2017.

7. See Airbnb, www.Airbnb.com, accessed August 25, 2017.

8. See, for example, https://www.volunteerhq.org/ and https://www.wearebamboo.com/. Bamboo has volunteer abroad programs specifically for people over 50 years old. www.abroadreviews.com is an independent entity that provides reviews of travel abroad programs.

9. James Hilton, *Lost Horizon* (London: Macmillan, 1933).

10. Cheryl Strayed, *Wild: From Lost to Found on the Pacific Coast Trail* (New York: Knopf, 2012).

11. For example, http://www.freetoursbyfoot.com/new-york-tours/, accessed July 13, 2017.

12. A good source is https://www.timeout.com/newyork.

13. The essay originally was published in *Holiday* magazine in 1949, and was re-released in book form in *Here Is New York* (New York: The Little Bookroom 1999).

14. Public Broadcasting Service, *POV*, http://www.pbs.org/pov/learning/photo-gallery-in-context/, accessed August 21, 2017.

15. Beryl Markham, *West with the Night: A Memoir* (New York: North Point, 2013).

16. Jack Kerouac, *On the Road* (New York: Viking Compass, 1957).

17. Paul Theroux, *The Great Railway Bazaar* (New York: Ballantine, 1975).

18. Guy Fieri, *Diners, Drive-ins and Dives: An All American Road Trip . . . With Recipes* (New York: HarperCollins, 2008).

19. Thinking Intelligent Food, http://www.intelligent-food.net/IF/LoveBeing. html, accessed August 24, 2017. Trisha started this website and used to blog about food and sustainable farming practices.

CHAPTER 6

1. National Institute on Aging, https://www.nia.nih.gov/alzheimers/publication/ preventing-alzheimers-disease/search-alzheimers-prevention-strategies, accessed July 1, 2017.

2. Iris Krasnow, *The LEAD Program*, http://iriskrasnow.com/lead/index.html, accessed August 24, 2017.

3. Krasnow, *The LEAD Program*.

4. Malcolm Gladwell, *Outliers: The Story of Success* (New York: Little, Brown, 2008).

5. The free podcast on iTunes is called *WPFW Inside Out*.

6. The *Inside Out* show is archived at www.wpfwfm.org. I generally host and produce the show on the first Tuesday of each month.

7. Formerly known as "Parents, Families, and Friends of Lesbians and Gays," PFLAG advances equality through its mission of support, education, and advocacy on behalf of people who are lesbian, gay, bisexual, transgender, and queer (LGBTQ); see www.Pflag.org, accessed August 24, 2017.

8. Maria Leonard Olsen, *Not the Cleaver Family—The New Normal in Modern American Families* (Mustang, OK: Tate, 2016).

9. My book talk at one of the largest literary festivals in the Washington metropolitan area was broadcast live on C-Span's Book TV; see www.c-span.org/ video/?427995-2/cleaver-family. I received honoraria to speak about my books at the Japanese American National Museum in Los Angeles and a race and gender conference in Tucson, among others.

10. William S. Burroughs, *Junky* (New York: Penguin, 1977).

11. *Montgomery County Journal* (ceased publication in 2005).

12. Quotation from Martin Niemöller on display in the Permanent Exhibition of the United States Holocaust Memorial Museum. Niemöller was a Lutheran minister who was later imprisoned for opposing Hitler's regime.

13. Jack Kornfield, *Time for Truth and Reconciliation*, https://jackkornfield.com/ time-for-truth-and-reconciliation, accessed August 20, 2017.

14. My books include *Mommy, Why's Your Skin So Brown?* (Milwaukee: Mirror, 2013); *Healing for Hallie* (Milwaukee: Mirror, 2016); *Not the Cleaver Family—The New Normal in Modern American Families* (Mustang, OK: Tate, 2016).

15. FreedomWithWriting.com (accessed August 24, 2017); AuthorsPublish.com (accessed August 31, 2017).

16. Viktor Frankl, *Man's Search for Meaning* (Boston: Beacon, 2006).

17. TaskRabbit, https://www.taskrabbit.com/about (accessed August 21, 2017).

18. The Verge, *Temping Fate: Can TaskRabbit Go from Side Gigs to Real Jobs?*, https://www.theverge.com/2013/5/23/4352116/taskrabbit-temp-agency-gig-econ omy (accessed August 21, 2017).

19. Airbnb, www.Airbnb.com (accessed August 25, 2017).

20. TaskRabbit, https://www.taskrabbit.com/taskrabbit-good (accessed August 21, 2017).

21. Madeleine Albright, *Prague Winter: A Personal Story of Remembrance and War, 1937–1948* (New York: Harper, 2012).

CHAPTER 7

1. Alzheimer's Association, https://www.alz.org/we_can_help_remain_socially _active.asp, accessed June 2, 2017.

2. Alzheimer's Association, 2017.

3. Clarissa Pinkola Estes, *Women Who Run with the Wolves: Myths and Stories of the Wild Woman Archetype* (New York: Ballantine, 1992).

4. Jahi Chikwendiu, "The Rhythm of the City: The Meridian Hill Park Drum Circle Evolves," *Washington Post*, August 28, 2014, https://www.washingtonpost .com/lifestyle/magazine/the-rhythm-of-the-city-the-meridian-hill-park-drum-circle -evolves/2014/08/27/ed2de94c-1e73-11e4-ab7b-696c295ddfd1_story.html?utm _term=.a60558b25ced, accessed June 15, 2017.

5. Susan Scafidi, *Who Owns Culture? Appropriation and Authenticity in American Law (New Brunswick, NJ: Rutgers University Press, 2005)*.

6. Gabrielle Bernstein, *Spirit Junkie: A Radical Road to Self-Love and Miracles* (New York: Harmony, 2012).

CHAPTER 8

1. Barbara Kantrowitz and Pat Wingert, *The Menopause Book* (New York: Work-man, 2009).

2. Author's interview of Pat Wingert, August 22, 2017.

3. WithLoveDC, http://www.withlovedc.com.

4. Meetups, https://www.meetup.com.

5. See Dan Buettner, *Thrive: Finding Happiness the Blue Zones Way* (Washington, D.C.: *National Geographic*, 2010).

6. Ed O'Brien, "Stop Putting Off Fun for After You Finish All Your Work," *Harvard Business Review*, July 7, 2017, https://hbr.org/2017/07/stop-putting-off-fun

-for-after-you-finish-all-your-work?utm_source=twitter&utm_medium=social&utm
_campaign=hbr, accessed July 11, 2017.

7. B. K. S. Iyengar, *Light on Life: The Yoga Journey to Wholeness, Inner Peace, and Ultimate Freedom* (London: Rodale, 2005).

8. WithLoveDC, www.withlovedc.com.

9. The organization Wanderlust currently has nearly 30 yoga triathlon events in cities around the world; https://wanderlust.com/108s/, accessed April 30, 2017.

10. Mayo Clinic, "Yoga: Fight Stress and Find Serenity," http://www.mayo-clinic.org/healthy-lifestyle/stress-management/in-depth/yoga/art-20044733?pg=1, accessed April 30, 2017.

11. Swami Satchidananda, *Jewels of Wisdom from the Teachings of Swami Satchidananda* (Buckingham, VA: Integral Yoga Publications).

12. Wanderlust, www.wanderlust.com.

13. Jeff Krasno, *Wanderlust—A Modern Yogi's Guide to Discovering Your Best Self* (New York: Rodale, 2015).

14. Lil Omm, http://lilomm.com/about-lil-omm/, accessed August 23, 2017.

15. Lil Omm, 2017.

16. Author's interview of Pleasance Silicki, August 30, 2017.

17. Interview of Pleasance Silicki, August 30, 2017.

18. ASPCA, "Shelter Intake and Surrender," https://www.aspca.org/animal
-homelessness/shelter-intake-and-surrender/pet-statistics, accessed April 30, 2017.

19. Tami Simon, *The Dharma of Dogs: Our Best Friends as Spiritual Teachers* (Boulder, CO: Sounds True, 2017).

20. Julia K. Vormbrock and John M. Grossberg, "Cardiovascular Effects of Human-Pet Dog Interactions," *Journal of Behavioral Medicine* 11, no. 5 (1988), 509–17, www.ncbi.nlm.nih.gov/pubmed/3236382, accessed April 30, 2017.

21. CBT helps individuals identify unhealthy, negative beliefs and behaviors and replace them with healthy, positive ones; http://www.mayoclinic.org/tests-procedures/
psychotherapy/details/what-you-can-expect/rec-20197200, accessed August 24, 2017.

22. DBT is a type of CBT that teaches behavioral skills to help individuals handle stress, manage emotions and improve relationships with others. http://www.
mayoclinic.org/tests-procedures/psychotherapy/details/what-you-can-expect/rec-20197200, accessed August 24, 2017.

23. Float Hopes, http://time.com/floating/.

24. Anette Kjellgren and Jessica Westman, "Beneficial Effects of Treatment with Sensory Isolation in Flotation-Tank as a Preventive Health-Care Intervention – A Randomized Controlled Pilot Trial," *BMC Journal of Complementary Alternative Medicine* 14 (2014), 417, https://www.ncbi.nlm.nih.gov/pmc/articles/PMC4219027/.

25. Justin Moyer, "Seeking Serenity? Flotation Therapy Offers an Inexpensive Way to Achieve It," *Washington Post*, September 23, 2013, https://www.washington post.com/opinions/seeking-serenity-flotation-therapy-offers-an-inexpensive-way-to
-achieve-it/2013/09/23/2882a8ac-d2ad-11e2-a73e-826d299ff459_story.html?utm
_term=.745d4175e3f2, accessed April 30, 2017.

26. Drake Baer, "Why NBA Star Steph Curry Uses a Sensory-Deprivation Tank to Recharge Every 2 Weeks," *Business Insider*, February 4, 2016, http://www.business

insider.com/steph-curry-is-obsessed-with-sensory-deprivation-tanks-2016-2, accessed April 30, 2017.

27. Hope Floats, https://www.hopefloatsusa.com.

CHAPTER 9

1. Tara Brach, www.TaraBrach.com.

2. See, for example, www.eOmega.org, www.IMCW.org, www.kripalu.org, and www.shambalamountain.org.

3. Some of my current favorite apps are Mindfulness, Insight Timer, Meditation Studio, Calm, and Take a Break.

4. *Grace and Frankie*, starring Jane Fonda and Lily Tomlin, premiered on Netflix in 2015.

5. Unitarian Universalist Association, The Seven Principles, http://www.uua.org/beliefs/what-we-believe/principles.

6. Alcoholics Anonymous, *Alcoholics Anonymous* (New York: Works Publishing, 1939), 85.

7. don Miguel Ruiz, *The Four Agreements: A Practical Guide to Personal Freedom (A Toltec Wisdom Book)* (San Rafael, CA: Amber-Allen, 1997).

8. don Miguel Ruiz, *The Four Agreements Companion Book: Using the Four Agreements to Master the Dream of Your Life (Toltec Wisdom)* (San Rafael, CA: Amber-Allen, 2000).

9. Ruiz, *Four Agreements Companion Book.*

10. Ruiz, *Four Agreements Companion Book.*

11. Ruiz, *Four Agreements Companion Book.*

12. Albert Camus, *The Myth of Sisyphus and Other Essays* (New York: Knopf, 1955).

13. Soul Purpose Productions, www.karmafest.com.

14. Marianne Williamson, *The Law of Divine Compensation: Mastering the Metaphysics of Abundance* (New York: HarperOne, 2012).

15. Brianna Sacks, "Reiki Goes Mainstream: Spiritual Touch Practice Now Commonplace in Hospitals," *Washington Post*, May 16, 2014, https://www.washingtonpost.com/national/religion/reiki-goes-mainstream-spiritual-touch-practice-now-commonplace-in-hospitals/2014/05/16/9e92223a-dd37-11e3-a837-8835df6c12c4_story.html?utm_term=.df0dd807f723, accessed August 23, 2017.

16. International Center for Reiki Training, http://www.reiki.org, accessed June 22, 2017.

17. See, for example, NIH Medline Plus, https://medlineplus.gov/magazine/issues/winter08/articles/winter08pg4.html, accessed August 23, 2017.

18. Womenade, http://www.washingtonwomenade.org/start.htm, accessed July 3, 2017.

19. World Kindness Movement, http://www.theworldkindnessmovement.org/about-us/, accessed August 23, 2017.

20. See http://www.miguelruiz.com.

21. Jessica Epperson-Lusty, www.evolvingmindfully.com, accessed August 23, 2017.

22. Jeanne Brumbaugh, *Helping Hearts Heal*, https://www.jeannebrumbaugh.com/, accessed August 20, 2017.

CHAPTER 10

1. Robert M. Pirsig, *Zen and the Art of Motorcycle Maintenance: An Inquiry into Values* (New York: Bantam, 1976).

2. Ann Patchett, *This is the Story of a Happy Marriage* (New York: HarperCollins, 2013), 97.

3. See Gary France, *France in America—A 21,000 Mile USA Discovery on my Harley-Davidson* (Shrove, Greencastle, Ireland: Inis Communications, 2013), www.garysfrance.com.

4. Indoor Skydiving Source, http://www.indoorskydivingsource.com/tunnels/.

5. P. J. Reece, "Ancient Tattoos: Theories of Heaven and Earth," vanishingtattoo.com, 2009, accessed May 7, 2017.

6. Conscious Ink has longer-lasting temporary tattoos of inspiring quotes and positive words; www.consciousink.com.

CHAPTER 11

1. Mel B., *Walk in Dry Places* (Center City, MN: Hazelden, 1996).

2. Virginia Woolf, *A Room of One's Own* (New York: Harcourt Brace, 1929).

3. The Southern Poverty Law Center maintains a listing and map of where hate groups like the Klan are active; https://www.splcenter.org.

4. *National Geographic*, "Nat Geo WILD: What Are the Odds? Some Surprising Shark Attack Stats," http://voices.nationalgeographic.com/2011/11/22/nat-geo-wild-what-are-the-odds-some-surprising-shark-attack-stats/.

5. NASA, "Follow the Water: Finding a Perfect Match for Life," https://www.nasa.gov/vision/earth/everydaylife/jamestown-water-fs.html.

6. Martha C. White, "Here's Proof Buying More Stuff Actually Makes You Miserable," *Time*, March 13, 2014, http://time.com/22257/heres-proof-buying-more-stuff-actually-makes-you-miserable/, accessed August 16, 2017 (citing Knox College psychology professor Tom Kasser's paper published in the journal *Motivation and Emotion*).

7. The Minimalists, http://www.theminimalists.com.

8. The Tiny Life, http://thetinylife.com.

9. The Money Wizard, www.mymoneywizard.com.

10. Shelley Emling and Damon Dahlen, "14 Women Show Off Wrinkles to Make a Potent Statement about Aging," *Huffington Post*, June 9, 2016, http://www.huffing

tonpost.com/entry/14-women-show-off-wrinkles-to-make-a-potent-statement
-about-aging_us_57560b50e4b0b60682deb823?section=women&.

11. Emling and Dahlen, "14 Women Show Off Wrinkles."

12. Jeff Galloway Training, http://www.jeffgalloway.com/training/run-walk/.

13. Viktor Frankl, *Man's Search for Meaning* (Boston: Beacon, 2006).

14. Jalal al-Din Rumi; see https://www.poets.org/poetsorg/poet/jalal-al-din-rumi.

15. Rhonda Byrne, *The Secret* (New York: Atria Books/Beyond Words, 2006).

PART III

1. David Steindl-Rast, "Want to Be Happy? Be Grateful." *TEDGlobal 2013*, https://www.ted.com/talks/david_steindl_rast_want_to_be_happy_be_grateful/, accessed November 26, 2017.

2. Steindl-Rast, "Want to Be Happy?"

3. Bronnie Ware, "The Top Five Regrets of the Dying" *Uplift*, February 3, 2016, http://upliftconnect.com/regrets-of-the-dying/, accessed July 12, 2017.

4. John O'Donohue, "For a New Beginning," in *To Bless This Space Between Us: A Book of Blessings* (New York: Doubleday, 2008).

5. There are many vision board workshops in the D.C. area, and are likely some near you or online. Making a vision board, however, can be as easy as cutting pictures and words out of old magazines, gluing or taping them to a poster or other surface, and keeping the finished board somewhere where you will see it often.

6. Steindl-Rast, "Want to Be Happy?"

Index

About the Author

Maria Leonard Olsen is a biracial woman whose parents were forbidden by law to marry in their home state of Maryland in the early 1960s. She is the mother of two children, a lawyer, journalist, and author. She leads writing/empowerment retreats for women, and is a cohost/producer of the *Inside Out* radio show on WPFW-FM, 89.3, in Washington, D.C. Maria graduated from Boston College and the University of Virginia School of Law, served in the Clinton administration's Department of Justice, fostered newborn babies awaiting adoption, and has been on the boards of Children's National Medical Center BOV, the Catholic Coalition for Special Education, the Alzheimer's Association of Greater Washington, and the GirlsUp Advisory Board. She has written for *The Washington Post*, *Washingtonian*, *Bethesda Magazine*, *Parenting*, *BabyTalk*, and *Washington for Women*. She recently returned to practicing law now that her children are launched. She wrote her first children's book, *Mommy, Why's Your Skin So Brown?*, about being mistaken for the nanny of her lighter-skinned children. *Healing for Hallie*, about the importance of expressing one's feelings, is her second children's book. *Not the Cleaver Family—The New Normal in Modern American Families*, exploring changes in the composition of American families during this past decade, was released in 2016. Maria has spoken at numerous schools and events, including the Mixed Remixed Festival in Los Angeles, the Japanese American National Museum's Family Day, the Washington Independent Review of Books, and the U.S. Department of Justice's Asian American Month Celebration (as the highest-ranking Asian American political appointee then at the Justice Department). Maria counsels women recovering from alcoholism, other addictions, and trauma. See www.Maria LeonardOlsen.com for additional information.